TOOLS AND TECHNOLOGY IN TRANSLATION

The Profile of Beginning Language Professionals in the Digital Age

1st Edition

RAFA LOMBARDINO
Published by Word Awareness

Word Awareness
P.O. Box 710099
Santee, CA 92072
www.WordAwareness.com

Printed in the United States of America

LOMBARDINO, Rafa.
Tools and Technology in Translation: The Profile of Beginning Language Professionals in the Digital Age / Rafa Lombardino

ISBN 978-1-5029974-4-9

1. Translation — Interpreting — Technology — Computer Tools. I. Lombardino, Rafa. II. Tools and Technology in Translation: The Profile of Beginning Language Professionals in the Digital Age.

October 2014
1st Edition

For more information about the book, visit
http://www.RafaLombardino.com/tools

TABLE OF CONTENTS

ACKNOWLEDGMENTS

This book would have never been possible without my Tools and Technology in Translation students. I have learned so much from them these past four years, and all these pages are dedicated to each one of them who had questions, feedback, and suggestions that allowed me to tailor the content to their needs and remind myself what it was like when I first started my career back in 1997.

By the same token, I'd also like to dedicate this book to my former instructors at the University of California, San Diego Extension—Mary Negrete, Gina Bushnell, Teri Newman, and Andy Benzo—for helping me overcome my irrational fear of speaking Spanish in public, fine-tuning my writing in English (especially those pesky prepositions!) and showing me the theory behind what I had already been practicing for seven years when I first enrolled in the program as a student. Thank you Mary Anderson, the former Program Representative who originally hired me, and Jennifer Eller, who took over the role and continues to provide the same great support to me and my fellow instructors. Thank you fellow instructors Jennifer De La Cruz, Judy Jenner, Carmen Alzas, and Rodolfo Valentán for the great talks during our yearly brunches and messages exchanged while I was writing this book.

I'd also like to thank my parents, Val and Nete, for listening to that eleven-year-old girl in her first English class in 5th grade back in Brazil. I was so fascinated by the experience of learning a new language that I probably pestered them until they enrolled me in an after-school program, so I could learn more. With all the books and tapes my dad would bring home I almost had a complete British accent, which I've long lost since moving to California, but his encouragement will always stay with me. And all the music videos with subtitled lyrics that my mom recorded on an old VCR while I was in school helped me study and improve my English skills more than she'll ever know. In all possible senses, I wouldn't be here if it weren't for their love and support.

Thanks, Darrell Champlin, for being my mentor back in Journalism School and showing me that it was possible to make a living as a translator. The six-month project we worked on together taught me so much about myself as a translator and was a strong foundation for me to find my comfort zone, daily output, and research skills. Thank you for trusting me and believing in my abilities.

A special thanks goes out to all my friends, both translators and non-translators, for the much needed insight during all the long talks—face-to-face or online—and for lending me an ear when I had hit a wall while working on a project or was trying to come up with different, creative ways to explain computer or translation matters to my students. Your feedback is always much appreciated and comforting. And you know exactly who you are! ;-)

Thanks, Jenn Grenier, for helping me compile the information about my student's current and future skills, for filling in as Project Manager, and acting as my copyeditor—both formally and informally—to help improve my writing.

Lastly, I must thank my husband and business partner, Vince, as well as our six-year-old Marissa and two-year-old Lorenzo, for putting up with me when the workload gets too heavy and I don't have a chance to step outside and work out a little so I can manage my stress levels. Their understanding, hugs, and kisses help me through the tough professional times, reminding me of what's really important in life: Our family.

Rafa Lombardino
October 2014

INTRODUCTION

This book is the result of a ten-week online class I started teaching back in 2010 as part of the Professional Certificate in English/Spanish Translation and Interpretation offered by the University of California San Diego Extension. Entitled "Tools and Technology in Translation," the purpose of the class is to provide practical advice about the technology and business side of our industry, thus complementing a very diversified curriculum that offers language-specific classes, theory and practice in translation, interpreting, sight translation, and different sessions that address specialized knowledge, such as business, legal and criminal proceedings, education, community, internal medicine and specialty medical areas, and simultaneous, consecutive, and court interpreting.

I myself studied towards this certificate between 2005 and 2008 and benefited from the great variety of theory and hands-on classes offered by the program. When the time came for Extension to expand the certificate and accommodate the demands and expectations of a more diversified demographic, they identified the need to offer a class that would focus on the routine of language professionals and share ideas on how to become more efficient by organizing resources, implementing tools to complete daily tasks, developing marketing strategies, and learning more about Computer-Assisted Translation (CAT).

And that was how "Tools and Technology in Translation" was conceived. I've been thoroughly enjoying the experience of teaching it and sharing some of the lessons I've learned—sometimes the hard way, by trial and error—so students can have a broader perspective of what it takes to set up their own language business or become part of a translation or interpreting team.

I've also learned a lot from my students, who are individuals coming from different walks of life, with a diversified professional and cultural background. They've opened my eyes to issues that beginners face nowadays, which more seasonal professionals might take for granted after years in the business or forget to reflect upon during their current fast-paced routine.

While the online class and, consequently this book, is mostly geared towards translators—those of us who work with the written language only—many of the ideas shared here will also prove to be useful to interpreters, especially those trying to break into the field or develop their business by marketing their services to a wider variety of potential clients.

In short, the main purpose of this book is to lift the curtain, look into what happens behind the scenes, and **address a crucial question that beginner translators and interpreters always ask themselves: "Do I have what it takes?"**

As we all know, being bilingual isn't enough to start working as a professional translator and/or interpreter and, throughout the UC San Diego Extension Program, instructors make all possible efforts to identify the niche that students could consider when putting their language skills to good use and not only build a solid business for themselves, but also help clients achieve their goals, in addition to serving the community as well.

As a secondary goal, I hope the contents shared here are useful to help established translators and interpreters, as well as educators, to **get a better idea on the profile of newcomers in the language industry, so we can better manage our mentoring efforts and help strengthen the T&I community.**

Rafa Lombardino
October 2014

A BRIEF HISTORY OF
TECHNOLOGY IN TRANSLATION

Sumerian literature is reportedly the first subject of translations known to mankind[1]. From the Middle Bronze Age through the Iron Age (27th to 6th centuries B.C.), literary works flourished in southern Mesopotamia, a region that today is the south of Iran, after Sumerians invented the first writing system. During the Akkadian Empire, and later the Babylonian Empire, these respective languages were imposed on the surrounding conquered states, but Sumerian continued to be used in literature and, consequently, translation into these two official languages was soon required. Much of what we know today as Babylonian literature is based on translations from earlier Sumerian works.

However, perhaps the most well-known translation dating back to ancient times was the Decree of King Ptolemy V, issued in 196 B.C. It was originally written in three languages: ancient Egyptian hieroglyphs (top), Demotic script (middle), and ancient Greek (bottom) and recovered on a stone slab known as the Rosetta Stone[2].

Other known examples of old translations include Buddhist scriptures called Lotus Sutra[3]—translated from Sanskrit to ancient Chinese by Dharmarakṣa, aka Zhu Fahu, in 286 AD—and the Old and New Testaments of the Bible—from Hebrew and ancient Greek into Latin, known as Vulgate, by St. Jerome

---

[1] TORRE, Esteban. *Teoría de la Traducción Literaria*, Síntesis, 1994.
[2] SOLÉ, Robert & VALBELLE, Dominique. *The Rosetta Stone: The Story of the Decoding of Hieroglyphics*, Four Walls Eight Windows, 2001 — Translation from the French by Steven Rendall.
[3] ZÜRCHER, E. *The Buddhist Conquest of China: The Spread and Adaptation of Buddhism in Early Medieval China*, Brill, 2005.

(Eusebius Hieronimus Sophronius)[4] at the end of the 4th century. It should be noted that St. Jerome was translating from two of the languages he learned only later in life into Latin, which was not his mother tongue—he spoke Illyrian and learned Latin after moving to Rome as a young man. Nevertheless, he became the Patron Saint of Translators and, in his honor, the International Translation Day was instituted by the International Federation of Translators (FIT) in 1953 and is celebrated September 30 on the feast of St. Jerome.

Until the advent of the press in (1040s in China and 1370s in Korea[5]), translators had to write by hand and copies were reproduced manually. Mechanical systems evolved around the 15th century with the Gutenberg Press[6], becoming increasingly smaller in size until typewriters, as we now know them, were invented in the mid-1800s[7], allowing translators to be more mobile. Throughout most of the 20th century, when typewriters became more affordable and some electric models hit the market, translating became a more widespread activity.

On the other hand, translators in the past could only rely on the knowledge they had acquired during their lives and on the information they could look up in books and dictionaries. In order to solve a vocabulary issue, they would need to communicate with an expert in another town, state or country, first by regular mail, and later by telephone.

Then there was a major breakthrough in technology that changed the rules of the game. Commercial computers reached

---

[4] WILLIAMS, Megan Hale. *The Monk and the Book: Jerome and the Making of Christian Scholarship*, University of Chicago Press, 2006.
[5] _____. *Printing* Press, Wikipedia: http://bit.ly/T3-WikiPress
[6] The Renaissance Secrets Team. *What Did Gutenberg Invent? — The Printing Process*, Open Learn, September 1st, 2005: http://bit.ly/T3-GutenbergPress
[7] ACOCELLA, Joan. *The Typing Life: How Writers Used to Write*, The New Yorker, April 9th, 2007: http://bit.ly/T3-TheTypingLife

the office in the 1950s[8] and translators, just like any other professional, had to learn an entire new set of skills to work more efficiently.

In the beginning, computers helped us to become more efficient because, besides the obvious improvement we had been enjoying from typing—which is a lot faster than writing by hand—we could also delete characters on the screen, as opposed to erasing them after they had already been printed on paper. Additionally, we could copy and paste contents within the same document and, later, among different files.

Soon systems were developed to help translators use databases that would aid them with terminology research. More interactive systems allowed translators to save their work in databases that would recall any previously-entered sentences in case repeated material arrived at their desks in the near future. And that was the beginning of Computer-Assisted Translation (CAT) tools.[9]

Yet another major breakthrough in technology changed the rules of the game one more time. The internet allowed people to connect themselves to an "information highway," access the World Wide Web, and soon interact with other people. Besides typing faster and being able to look up terminology and back up their work, translators are now able to get in touch, in real time, with people a world apart that can help them solve their translation issues.

Likewise, the internet brought translators and clients together. We are no longer confined to a 9-to-5 job at a translation agency or the language bureau of a large corporation, or, as an alternative, working as a freelancer for local clients.

[8] _____. *How the Computer Changed the Office Forever*, BBC, July 31st, 2013: http://bit.ly/T3-OfficeComputers

[9] COCCI, Lucia. *CAT Tools for Beginners*, Translation Directory: http://bit.ly/T3-CATBeginner

Translators can now set up their own business, market their services, and work from home or anywhere with internet access.

Translators no longer receive hundreds of printed pages a year sent by regular mail or fax. It's all done by email, FTP servers or services that store files "in the cloud." Neither do we have to send resumes left and right looking for an opportunity of stable employment. We can apply for different projects individually and truly decide when we work, what we work on, and whom we work with. Or, better yet, we can now set up a virtual office and potential clients will be able find us online doing a simple web search.

For translators living abroad, in a country where their mother tongue isn't mainstream, the internet becomes an invaluable resource in keeping up to date with how their own language evolves. We can read books and news articles, listen to the radio, and even watch TV online to access the same information and be in contact with the same everyday expressions used in our country of origin.

The same is true for translators who do not live in a country where their source language is spoken and now, more than ever, we can have access to the same discourse that native speakers of our B language have at their disposal. This allows translators to keep up with how their second language evolves, what new expressions are being incorporated into everyday talk—mostly thanks to pop culture—and how technical terms are used by people working in the respective fields.

In a nutshell, being a translator in the age of technology means working anywhere, anytime, and with whomever we choose. It's not only about being language experts, but knowing our computers well enough to work with them in harmony. Being a translator is being a researcher, too, and knowing where to find more information about context and language use. It's being an entrepreneur and, literally, minding your own business.

Let's review how technology has helped translators become more efficient:

✓ We have become faster because we can type our translations and edit them on the fly.

✓ We can back up our work, in case we're assigned similar jobs in the future, thus minimizing the need for repeated work.

✓ We can research terminology not only within preset databases, but with human-to-human interactions, and keep up with the evolution of our working languages.

✓ We can network in real time with clients and colleagues alike, regardless of where they are.

✓ We can set up a virtual office to advertise our services and be reachable by potential clients.

THE ROLE OF TRANSLATORS
IN A TECHNOLOGICAL AGE

Technology is not an option in today's professional world; it is a necessity. As a translator, you must accept this truth and make a proactive effort to learn about the tools that will improve your efficiency and help you complete each task the best possible way. After all, think about other professionals—physicians, engineers, teachers, etc.—whose work has evolved due to technology. Why would it be any different in the translation industry?

With that in mind, you must also accept that each new technology requires new investments, which is not only the price you pay for a tool, but also the time it takes for you to learn how to use it.

Here are some ideas on how technology makes the life of translators a little easier:

- **Mobility (aka Telecommuting)** — You only need an internet connection to keep in touch with clients and colleagues and receive/submit files.

- **Email Exchanges** — Communication in real time, which allows you to cut down the time you need to evaluate potential projects and provide clients with a quote.

- **Web Networking** — The world is now your oyster and you're not limited to your local contacts anymore; you may advertise your services online to find international clients and rely on the collaboration of colleagues who are on the other side of the world.

Once you understand the importance that technology currently has in the life of a translator, you can start to reflect on the role that translators play in the world. Here are some ideas:

- **Socio-Political Aspect** — We help different cultures and governments understand each other, thus establishing communication between nations.

- **Commercial Aspect** — We help companies sell their products and services to foreign markets, in addition to contributing to training their workers in international branches, so they can follow corporate policies and assure quality throughout the entire process.

- **Globalization Aspect** — We are able to *localize* messages (adapting them to the reality of the target audience) or *internationalize* materials (generalizing them to address multiple target audiences.)

More than ever, now that we are in the 21st century, language professionals are able to become protagonists in how the world turns. Translators and interpreters are part of the relief team when a natural disaster strikes, we help scientists and the academia in general spread the word about new studies and discoveries, we assist in times of war and during the peacemaking process, we help communities integrate immigrants into the fabric of society, and erase the geographical borders and language limitations of international literature.

In the next few pages, let's reflect on the work translators do to contribute to the world's progress and how you, as a language professional, can enter the T&I industry or further your participation in it.

GETTING TO KNOW
YOURSELF AS A TRANSLATOR

No matter what career we wish to pursue, knowing ourselves is key to becoming successful in what we do. That is what makes us aware of our strengths and what we need to develop in order to improve and grow as a professional.

In the translation field in particular, we need to combine speed and accuracy in order to keep clients pleased with the great quality we have to offer, while also keeping ourselves happy by organizing our schedule to complete all our projects on time—there's always a deadline right around the corner!—and have time to relax and enjoy life.

In this fast-paced industry, being able to streamline our activities to meet tight deadlines is equal to having good survival instincts and skills. Yet translators must work responsibly, without rushing our projects, in order to assure quality and keep a good reputation.

Needless to say, being fast doesn't mean being quick and negligent, but efficient and effective.

Much has already been said about the language-related competencies required of translators. We all know we must speak at least two languages very well and at a formal level. We must be aware of grammar rules, correct spelling, and writing styles. We need to take register into account, that is, the language that the author used when writing the source document, so that we keep it at the same level for our target audience, thus being true to the message and word choices.

Apart from that, what other things do you have to reflect about when considering the idea of becoming a translator? Since our main focus here is technology and business practices, let's explore some issues you must anticipate while interacting with your computer and streamlining your work in order to maximize your efficiency.

HOW COMFORTABLE ARE YOU
WITH YOUR COMPUTER SKILLS?

As mentioned in the previous section, there's no fighting technology when you're a translator. Just keep in mind that you don't have to be a tech guru and master every aspect of the computer world. What is crucial, though, is that you master your work tools, so that you become the most efficient translator you can be.

For now, **there's not much you can do about feeling comfortable around technology than playing with your computer yourself**. If you stop to think about it, nobody can really teach you how to use a computer, because it all depends on what you use it for. Even if two people need to perform the same task, odds are they'll select different tools and methods to achieve the same goal.

In other words, people who have different personal and professional needs will use computers differently. The most important thing is for you to find what your computer has to offer in your field or activity and then implement it and practice as much as you can to become familiar with these tools and comfortable with your own set up.

o   **What Computer Should I Buy?**

There's really no answer to that. You can listen to different professionals, ask questions to several sales representatives, and all you'll get is multiple—often conflicting—answers. What may work for some, may not work for you. However, there are some "universal truths" to working with computers as a translator.

First of all, you need something fast. That means you should invest in processing power. If your processor has a higher capacity, you'll be able to have multiple programs open at the same time without experiencing any lag. And, if you're planning on using a CAT tool, your random-access memory (RAM) will also be crucial for your computer to look up information on multiple databases (translation memories as well as glossaries) and present it to you as quickly as possible, so you can go on researching and translating.

Second of all, **do your homework. That means looking up the programs you'll potentially use and reading their system requirements**, including screen resolution, RAM, and operating system, among other specific details.

Storage capacity remains important as well, but you don't have to worry about it as much as we used to in the past. If your hard drive only has room for so many bytes, you can always buy an external hard drive—and put your backup skills to practice— or look into cloud storage solutions, which means that your files are stored and/or backed up in an on-line location.

This is a very attractive option if you work with multiple computers (i.e. a desktop and a laptop,) so there is no need to transfer files between them (i.e. emailing them to yourself or saving them to a USB drive) because your content will always be accessible online once you log into your remote service.

Another part of this debate is whether you should get a Mac or a PC. It really is a personal question that only you could answer. The only thing you must keep in mind is that some software is not universal; what runs on one operating system may not work on another—not without some extra help, that is.

Some CAT tools and other programs that may assist you (i.e. electronic dictionaries or accounting software) were designed especially for a Microsoft environment and, if you use a Mac or Linux machine, you'll need something known as an "emulator" in order to trick the program into thinking you do have a PC with a version of Microsoft installed. Or, as an alternative, you can have a virtual machine inside your regular computer.

For example, I run a Linux Ubuntu machine with a virtual machine that runs Windows 7, since my accounting software and main glossary program are made for Windows only. However, I enjoy the convenience of avoiding known bugs and viruses that target Windows computers and, in the event that something goes wrong with my virtual machine, I can always remove it and install it again, because my files and main operations (email, web surfing, CAT tool, file system) remain up and running on my Linux computer.

But, don't worry! Both emulators and virtual machines are legitimate options that won't turn you into a hacker who is doing something illegal. All you need to do is purchase the required software and pay for their licenses accordingly, while enjoying the convenience of having all your tools at the same location. It does, however, take extra steps to set things up and, sometimes, a little bit of expert knowledge to make everything work.

○   **Desktop vs. Laptop**

Of course one of the most attractive things about being a translator is mobility, or being able to work anywhere. That's called "telecommuting," or the ability to work online without the need to commute to a physical office. Thinking about that, a laptop would be ideal for you to take your work on the go, correct? Well, things aren't always black and white...

On the one hand, it's good to have a laptop as an option in case your desktop is down for maintenance. That way you minimize your downtime and can keep working on your current projects. On the other hand, desktops are still a more stable option, while laptops can be more fragile, unstable and prone to accidents, in addition to getting outdated faster.

Maybe a better way of thinking about this dilemma isn't asking yourself whether you should have a desktop or a laptop, but rather what your plan B would be if you only had one or the other. So, if it is within your budget, you should definitely take advantage of the convenience laptops have to offer. However, the safest thing is that you don't rely solely on it, because there are several things that can go wrong.

Nevertheless, you should always backup your work, no matter the type of machine you use, so plan ahead to avoid headaches in a moment of crisis. **Redundancy is actually a good thing when working with technology.**

> **Things you should consider when working on a laptop:**
>
> ✓ They're more exposed to physical damage, since they're more mobile than the stationary computer that sits on a desk all the time.
>
> ✓ Laptop parts are more expensive because they may have been designed especially for that model.
>
> ✓ Their lifespan is usually shorter and some manufacturers may discontinue support to old models, which means hardware components will no longer work correctly if there is a bug.

○ **Typing vs. Dictating**

Do you type slowly? Well, there are a couple of things you can do about it.

First of all, try out one of those websites that test your typing speed and practice, practice, practice. Your brain is like a muscle, and it will get stronger if you exercise it. Yes, your hands are the ones doing the typing, but you must train your brain to tell your fingers where to go. So, get to know your keyboard better, see where all the keys are laid out, and follow typing exercises to finally master the typing-while-looking-at-the-screen speed.

Now, if you're more of a talker than a typist, consider investing in a speech-recognition tool that you can train to follow your speaking patterns, so you can dictate your translation and save on keyboard and mouse use. If your brain is wired that way and can communicate faster with your mouth than it does with your fingertips, you'll greatly benefit from dictation and avoid potential repetitive strain injury (RSI).

Whether you follow one method or the other, **take the necessary precautions to keep your instrument healthy**. Do strengthening and stretching exercises not to feel any discomfort in your hands, elbows, shoulders, and neck after typing for long hours. If you're taking advantage of dictation, do some facial stretching exercises to relax your jaw and cheekbones, take good care of your vocal cords, and drink lots of water, too.

- ○ **Ergonomics 101**
Knowing how to work well with your computer isn't only about learning the specs, mastering the programs you will use, and what tools and methods work for you. It's also about setting up a work environment to maximize productivity and comfort.

    Before decorating your home office, make sure you learn the basics about ergonomics and select a desk and chair that are comfortable to your height and body type. Consider purchasing a better monitor if yours is old or very small. Look into ergonomic keyboard options and wrist rests that will help you keep your hands and arms at a good angle and position.

    You should also schedule breaks to stretch, look away from your screen and give your brain enough time to reset, so you don't get stuck in your current task and can find language solutions more effectively. Try to **work regular physical activities into your schedule** as well, which will not only keep you in shape, but also help you cope with stress, and give your mind a much-deserved rest.

SPEED IS KEY IN THE TRANSLATION INDUSTRY

Once again, being "fast" doesn't mean rushing things and delivering a project that is far from accurate. In this field, speed means working efficiently and identifying shortcuts to finish a task or find correct answers quickly. **If you're organized, you will definitely both your goals: being accurate and on time.**

Knowing your average output is one of the most important things translators can do in the technological age. While some may say that it's impossible to know exactly how many words you are able to translate in a given hour, considering the several variables that go into each project, there is always a way to estimate your production once you know yourself better. Believe me, I've been doing exactly that since 1997!

Did I start out knowing how much work I'd be able to complete every day? Of course not, but I had to start somewhere. And there are many people out there who, like me, are able to plan their day around their projects, thus securing a reputation of being a responsible professional and assuring client loyalty.

By finding their average output, many professionals have been able to organize their schedule and line up projects based on this key information about their own routine (read more about average output at the end of this subsection.)

o   **Organize Your Schedule**

The best way to stay organized is to find a tool that works for you, period! Whether you like writing things down on a daily planner or white board, or you're like me and can no longer live without your online calendar, you'll only benefit from having a visual aid to tell you how your day or week is going.

First of all, if you're working from home, try to **establish your office hours**. Since you're a freelancer, you are able to work whenever you want, which doesn't mean "whenever you feel like it," so try to make it as consistent as possible to stay on track and help your clients know when you'll be available to assist them throughout the week. It's also a good idea to check any time zone differences, so you and your clients on the other side of the world are on the same page as far as your availability.

Make a habit of writing down or typing everything related to your professional efforts. Did you spend three hours working on a translation for a client? Did you spend one hour updating your resume and/or online profile? Did you spend half an hour browsing for a cool logo to finally put a business card together?

Keep track of what you do not only to organize yourself and plan your schedule, but also to identify any unwanted "time warps" in your day, such as spending too much time on tasks that don't contribute to your short-term goals—that is delivering your current projects on time.

✓ **REMEMBER: You will only be able to improve your daily routine and become more efficient and effective if you have sufficient data to make the necessary adjustments. Establish a calendar system to see exactly where your professional efforts are going. This way, you'll also be able to schedule tasks that are not related to translation work, but crucial for you to manage your career and grow.**

---

o **Allocate Time For Clerical Duties**

If you keep a calendar or daily planner, you'll be able to look at the available time slots and fit in tasks that are not exactly translation-related. It also serves the purpose of scheduling your breaks during a long translation project to let your brain rest for a while, especially if you're looking for inspiration for that word or expression that got you stuck.

When you have a translation business, besides spending time translating, researching, and proofreading (i.e. translation work itself,) you'll also need to manage your time to accomplish all the other tasks that revolve around your main activity.

For example, you need to get back to clients who have emailed you to check your availability for an upcoming project, which you better do sooner, rather than later, in order to say "yes" or "no" to new work. **Replying promptly is a sign of good customer service**, but stopping what you're doing every five minutes to answer messages is actually counterproductive. So, here are two suggestions to solve this issue:

1) Check the program or web interface you use to set up an email alert option, which will trigger a pop-up window or a little notice on the corner of your screen to let you know you've received a new message. That way, you can set your priorities and reply to what is really important (e.g. a new project from a current client.) Some things can be addressed in a couple of hours (e.g. a request for information from a potential client,) while replies to mass emails can be combined in 30-minute windows (e.g. a message from a job board or agency about a new project in your language pair and/or field of expertise.)

2) Reply to emails around the smaller projects that you completed within 30-60 minutes, or take breaks every hour when working on a large project, so you'll get back to clients within enough time and enjoy a quick break before resuming your work or moving on to the next project on your schedule.

✓ QUICK TIP: Suggestion # 2 is good to get a boost of productivity, because breaks help your brain rest before refocusing on a project. Otherwise, you may end up looking at the clock every five minutes and feeling you're not making much of a progress.

Other tasks you can label as "**clerical duties**" include keeping your **accounting** books updated, so you can **issue invoices** and **collect payment** for your hard work. And you need to **balance your bills**, too. On the more proactive side, you'll need to **review your resume and online profiles** periodically, to make sure they're up to date, in addition to **contacting potential clients** and **looking through job boards** for projects that may match your skills. As for the technological aspect, there will always be countless **computer and software updates** and **file backups**, which you sure don't want to get caught up doing when you have a document to deliver.

If you plan ahead, things will go a lot smoother, so find the system that works for you and start working on your to-do list.

○   Spend Less Time Researching Terminology

Speed is not only about typing fast, but **knowing where to go to solve translation issues** that will come your way, so you don't waste too much time researching less reliable sources.

If you already have an area of expertise in mind, research specialized dictionaries to add to your shopping list. You should also find websites from associations and organizations dealing with the relevant area, as well as universities with programs related subjects, because odds are they have publications that will help you find valuable descriptions for terminology you may come to use. These are example of the reputable sites you'll resort to in order to complement your terminology research, so bookmark their URLs for quick access.

Start working on a glossary, so you have keywords ready and your respective translation according to context and register. Some people like managing spreadsheets with manually-entered terms. Others decide to manage their terminology using databases, such as the ones provided by CAT tools. Either way, you can go beyond documenting terms in your A and B languages. Depending on the solution you choose, you can add definition, examples, and links to relevant articles, images or other resources.

All these ideas represent ways to centralize your preferred terminology, so you'll know where to find answers.

> ✓ **REMEMBER: Be proactive and try to anticipate what you will need to do during a "live project," then work towards addressing these issues before they actually become a problem. This will only increase your efficiency.**

o **Make an Informed Decision on Computer-Assisted Translation (CATs) Tools**

Being a fast translator nowadays is also related to using **CAT tools**, which **help us manage both the material we have translated and our glossaries** in order to cut down the time we spend translating similar documents and researching terminology over and over again.

For the sake of improving speed and output, keep in mind that this very relevant tool has the ability to make you spend less time typing because it will remember sentences you've translated in the past and show you suggested translations based on your previous work. It can definitely go a long way when you're working with the same clients over and over, since the potential for repeated material increases greatly.

While you have some downtime in the beginning of your career, put some time aside to try out the 30-day free trials offered by many of the CAT tools available in the market. As mentioned earlier, you need to find what works for you and "play" with your computer to become more familiar with program functionalities and learn what it can do for you.

o **Find your Average Pace in Words per Hour/Day**

Finally, once you organize your schedule and find the most comfortable way for you to put words on the page, the next thing you could do is **start timing yourself**. If you don't currently have "live projects" that real clients have assigned to you, use news articles to practice and document your progress. The most important thing now is to **keep track of how much you can translate within a given period of time**.

Start by estimating the amount of words you're able to translate in one hour, because that's the smallest unit of measure for your average output: **words per hour (WPH)**. You can then multiply it by the number of hours you're willing to work every day and get your approximate daily output. The same goes for weekly and monthly capacity.

Once again, this calculation is just an approximation, because many things come into play once you start working on a project, and there's always the possibility of unforeseen circumstances:

a) **Text-Related Variables** — Level of difficulty of a given text, more or less time spent researching and proofreading.

b) **Computer-Related Variables** — Malfunction, forced maintenance or updates.

c) **Human-Related Variables** — How you feel on a given day, if someone in your household needs attention, or a friend of relative decides to call or stop by to chat.

✓ **QUICK TIP: Practicing with news articles will help you learn what kind of subjects you feel more comfortable with. If you're familiar with the lingo in a given field, odds are you'll research fewer keywords because the specialized terminology is already part of your vocabulary.**

Your average output will give you a rough idea of how long it will take you to get the job done, so you **don't overschedule, overpromise and underdeliver**.

For example, if your client sends you a 2,000-word document and you realize you're able to translate 250 words per hour, it would take you at least eight hours to get it done. If you put a couple more hours on top of that, just to be on the safe side, you'd need a total ten hours. Let's say you work five-hour days; that means you'd tell the client that they would have the project back within at least 48 hours.

However, should anything happen and you have a legitimate reason to ask for a deadline extension, make sure you contact your client as soon as you identify the issue. And for "legitimate reason" I mean if you got ill, had a family emergency, or something beyond your control happened (e.g. computer crashes, loss of power, natural disasters, etc.)

Always use your best judgment before you decide to ask for an extension, because it should really be a last-resort solution—not a way out for procrastination or bad planning.

As I mentioned before, right now the idea of having an "average output" may sound either challenging or outrageous to you if you haven't been working with translations on a regular basis. But, believe me, after so many years in the industry, many colleagues and I can testify to that. Knowing yourself and organizing your schedule will greatly help you find the "magic" WPH number that works for you.

YOU MUST REALLY
MIND YOUR OWN BUSINESS

Many translators either start working in the field because they need a second source of income or wish to switch careers. Sometimes, it's something they stumble upon because they already have a good set of language skills. Others seek formal education before taking a plunge into the industry and, while most beginners have the theory and technique down, they may not be really sure where to go to turn their language skills into a professional and profitable business. Here's one big tip: just **go on line, because the world is your oyster!**

You can work as a freelancer under your own name or initials, being classified either as an independent contractor or a sole proprietor. You can team up with a colleague to create a partnership. Or you can establish a corporation that will either employ other individuals or hire freelance language talents on a regular basis to address your clients' translation needs.

In this section, we'll talk about how technology can help you **set up your business** and deal with the "headaches" that inevitably become a side effect of being an independent contractor: invoicing, bookkeeping, accounting, collecting payments, solving legal issues, and filing your taxes.

Another aspect of being an independent contractor is working on your **negotiation skills**. You most likely will not have a boss or manager to assign tasks to you on a daily or weekly basis, so you must learn more about yourself as a professional, find your comfort zone, and identify the rates you'll charge, how fast you can deliver a project and—most importantly—what your own limitations are in order to turn down projects you won't be able to complete.

We'll also discuss how to **work with project managers** and managing projects yourself when you need to **bring in some trusted colleagues** to get the job done on time and effectively.

Before we start talking about what it takes to build a business from the ground up, it's important to highlight the fact that not everyone may be cut out to be a business owner and act like their own boss. Some people work better when they have a structure laid out for them, instead of taking care of it themselves—and there's nothing wrong with that. **The main thing here is to reflect on what's ahead of you as a freelancer and potential business owner, so you can decide if that option is right for you, or if working for a translation agency or the language bureau of a large corporation is a better match to your personality and expectations.**

The upside of having your own business is that you are your own boss, set your own schedule, and make executive decisions on which projects you'll take on and how you'll expand your operations. The downside of it is that you'll have to wear many hats and take different responsibilities that don't only involve sitting down and getting to work on a translation project.

Following, you'll find some ideas on where to start and some issues you need to anticipate when considering all your options before you go into business for yourself. The only thing I ask you to keep in mind while reading the next few topics is that these are lessons drawn from my own experience, as well as from the experiences of colleagues with whom I've interacted throughout these years.

The suggestions below should <u>NOT</u> be construed as legal, financial, accounting, tax, or medical advice, so it's best to look for a professional to discuss your particular details and the legislation, regulations, and norms currently in effect in your country.

---

o   **Set up a Business Plan**

So, you decided to go into business for yourself. Congratulations! Now, roll up your sleeves and get to work on the foundation for your business. That way, you will be able to start operating in a structured manner and grow towards your short- and long-term goals.

The purpose of having a business plan is getting a general idea of what you want to accomplish. Keep in mind that nothing is set in stone and your goals may change as you become more active in the translation industry. Nevertheless, putting some thought into a plan will give you a direction and help you prioritize and make adjustments along the way.

> **Check the EXTRAS in this book for a Business Plan Draft you can use to brainstorm what you want from your business.**

Start by laying out your short-term goals. Maybe you're currently working on a degree or thinking about becoming a member of a professional association. These are things you could set yourself to accomplish within the first five years of your career.

If you're very ambitious, look into some graduate programs to work towards your master's degree or PhD, thus furthering your specialization. Maybe you would like to add another source language to your list... If you plan for it now, you can start taking classes to develop or improve your skills and consume media (books, newspapers and magazines, music, movies, etc.) in your desired new source language so, in about ten years, this would be yet another combination you could offer your clients.

Once you've brainstormed your goals, you can get into more practical things. What will the name of your business be? Write down a few ideas and then look them up online to make sure they haven't been taken already. Try similar combinations (e.g. singular/plural forms) just to be on the safe side. You should come up with something unique that can bring a strong image and slogan to mind when clients think about your business.

One you have a few options, envision your logo. That will be your visual representation. Remember that one image is worth a thousand words! When people look at your logo, they should think about you and your services right away. And, to tie it all together, come up with a catchy slogan that summarizes the purpose of your business.

Next, move on to your mission statement, which can be a more elaborated paragraph about what your business will offer clients and how you will set out to do so. If you're planning on having a website and want to apply for a Better Business Bureau (BBB) accreditation, one of their requirements is that you state your business mission on your website.

Now, try to visualize your target audience. Think about your source and target language(s) and field(s) of expertise. Who would be interested in hiring your services? And who will benefit from your work?

Lastly, list all the marketing materials you would like to create to promote your business. More on that in *Section 3: Selling Your Professional Services.*

o   **Make an Informed Decision on your Business Status**

Now that you have a clearer image of what you would like your business to be, let's talk about how to effectively set it up. But, before we move on, I'd like to make it clear that the information related to this item is focused on the current reality in the United States and based on my own personal experiences establishing a partnership back in 2004 and then running a small corporation since 2009. In other words, the specifics about establishing a business will relate to what a translator living in the USA may go through, so if you live in another country, try to take the general idea of structuring your business, which is universal, and learn more about the legislation and regulations in your own country in order to obtain a business license.

Your first option as a translator or interpreter is acting as a self-employed individual, that is, a **freelancer** working under your own name.

You can create a **Sole Proprietorship**, meaning that you are personally liable for all your business profits and losses. You pay taxes on your total income and—let's hope it never happens!—if your business is in debt or sued, your personal assets will come into play. That means risking your car, house and other possessions to pay for your business expenses, so take a moment to reflect on that.

The same is true for a **Partnership**, but you don't have to do it alone: two or more partners can share profits and losses. With that in mind, choose your partners well. You must share the same goals and agree on how you'll operate in order to prevent any issues that can put the partnership in jeopardy due to disagreement between the partners.

When you're looking into **Corporate** options (S Corp or C Corp,) things start to change, because the business becomes its own "person." As we'll see later on in this section, your company can retain its own assets after paying employees, taxes and business expenses.

Especially with a **Limited-Liability Company (LLC)**, the individual is protected and only the company assets come into play in the extreme event that the business is sued, for example. A **Limited Liability Limited Partnership (LLLP)** works similarly with general partners and limited partners.

I understand this is a lot of information to process and our goal here is to present it superficially so that you know what's out there according to United States laws. Once again, the best thing for you is to sit with a lawyer or paralegal professional who specializes in the field, so you can discuss what works best for you and get everything ready to file all the required paperwork to establish your business.

From a client's perspective, not much changes on their end if they're dealing with a freelancer or a company providing language services. The decision to switch from a self-employed individual to another business status may be triggered by tax reasons, though. The way your income is taxed will change dramatically according to your status as a service provider.

Check the EXTRAS in this book for links to more in-depth explanations on each type of business setup and some of the forms you need to file in the United States.

LEGAL PAPERWORK

In addition to all the paperwork you'll need to file in order to establish your business—either it is a "Doing Business As" form or documents required of a corporation—let's talk briefly about some legal paperwork you may have to sign while working as a language service provider.

o   **Internal Revenue Service Forms**

No matter whether you are a freelancer, partnership or corporation, if you're established in the USA and work with U.S. clients, you will need to fill out a W9 with your personal information and receive 1099s when it's time for tax season.

First of all, regardless of your location, you must always send clients an **invoice** with your data, project description, and relevant payment details. They will accept a simple document or spreadsheet as an invoice, but I highly recommend that you send them non-editable PDFs to make sure nobody changes your information—it's always better to be safe than sorry. We'll talk more about invoices, collecting payment, and income taxes later on under **Financial Issues**.

So, before you send U.S. clients your first invoice, they'll most likely request that you fill in a **W9** form, or **Request for Taxpayer Identification Number and Certification**, which was created by the United States government through the Internal Revenue Service (IRS), so that U.S. persons—both citizens and residents paying income tax in the country—can provide their information to companies they contribute to as a self-employed individual or a business providing services to another business.

You'll need to fill in your name, address, Social Security Number (SSN) or Employer Identification Number (EIN), and banking information (for direct deposit payment, if applicable) so that your client can make payments to you and issue a 1099 in the beginning of the following year.

And that takes us to the **1099** form, which is another IRS form filed by your client's company with copies to the State Tax Department and the Recipient (in this case, you) containing information on how much they paid out in **miscellaneous income to an individual who is not a company employee.**

So this is basically what happens when you work as a translator or interpreter in the United States:

1) You fill out a W9 with your information when you first start working with a company.

2) You provide a service and then send an invoice when the project is completed.

3) Come tax season, you'll receive a copy of the 1099 your client must send to the IRS with the total amount they paid you during the previous year.

○ Vendor Agreement

It is a basic contract to formalize the relationship between you and your client. It will identify both parties and most likely make it pretty clear that you're a service provider, not an employee of the company in question. This is expected, since the company hiring your services doesn't want you to claim any rights or benefits that are reserved to employees only. Simply put, you will be acknowledging that you are providing a service on an as-needed basis and, consequently, are not entitled to a monthly salary, health insurance and retirement package.

This will also be the document that specifies payment terms, such as how many days the client will make payment after an invoice is issued, as well as what payment method will be used. Most agreements also cover penalties applicable to service providers who don't meet their deadlines, such as deduction on total payment.

If your client does not provide you with a similar document and there is a potential for you two to establish a long-term collaboration, I highly recommend that you have a contract ready and request that your clients sign it before you provide services to them.

> **Check the EXTRAS in this book for links to agreement templates.**

o **Non-Disclosure Agreement**

As the name indicates, it is a legal document you sign to ensure that you will **not disclose any information** you receive while providing services to your client. This is especially important if you need to translate **business secrets**, such as information about your client's products or services, which are of a **highly confidential nature**. In other words, you can't talk about the translation you're providing to your client, because it may reveal **proprietary data** on how they conduct their business, thus exposing your client's company to competitors.

o **Non-Compete Agreement**

This type of agreement is signed mostly between language service providers and translation agencies in order to ensure that a translator will not contact an end client directly and try to get their business and cut the middle man (i.e. the translation agency) out of the equation.

It is worth mentioning here that, no matter how badly your relationship with a translation agency may turn out to be, you should **NEVER** try to approach their contacts with the intention to steal their clients and, worse yet, bad mouth the translation agency itself or its project managers. That will only reflect poorly on your own business practices and ethics.

The best thing you can do when you face this situation is to stop working with the agency you're unhappy with and invest in your own marketing to find quality clients yourself.

FINANCIAL ISSUES

As mentioned above, being an independent translator or interpreter and running your own business means more than simply working on translation and interpreting. You must make sure that you fill in all **legal requirements** and have your **finances up to date** for things to go smoothly.

Here is some general insight on how things work, but make sure you look into your particular case and surround yourself with professionals in order to make it work and avoid major headaches down the road.

o **Receiving Payments and Filing Income Taxes**

If you plan on accepting payments made out to you personally, you shouldn't need to file any extra paperwork. Clients will make checks payable to you and you'll deposit it into your bank account, as any other check.

However, for the sake of keeping things separate, I highly recommend that you open a bank account for business purposes only. In that case, you may want to file for a "**Doing Business As**" name, also known as DBA. That way, you would have a separate business account for "John Smith Translations" or "J.S. Language Services," for example.

Likewise, I also recommend that you talk to a **lawyer or paralegal professional** if you're planning on doing something as simple as filing for a DBA, because there may be other paperwork involved in the process that you are unaware of. And, believe me, you don't want to learn that you missed a city permit three years ago, when you first started working under your business name, and now you have to pay late fees on it...

Now, assuming that business has been running smoothly for some months and you've been depositing payments to your account, let's say that you made $30,000 the previous year while working as a translator. When the time comes for you to report your income, if you're working as a **self-employed individual**, you must report those $30,000 and, from my own experience, this miscellaneous income ends up being heavily taxed. This is due to the fact that you have not paid any mandatory contributions on it when payments were first made to you.

On the other hand, if you own a company, you would be considered your company's employee and, for example, pay yourself a salary of $2,000 a month in order to claim a yearly income of $24,000 as an individual. If you set up your salary correctly, through a payroll system, your company is already paying employee taxes and social security on your paycheck, as any employer does when they pay their employees.

The remaining $6,000 from that $30,000 earned throughout the year is then classified as your **company assets**. This money belongs to your company and is used to pay for your business bills and corporate taxes. Then, whatever is leftover could be reinvested into your business to improve it.

For example, you can invest it by putting it into a business savings account or contributing to a financial plan to make your money work for you. You also have the option of paying yourself a bonus, for example, which would then be added to your personal income tax.

Of course, the explanation above is oversimplified just to tap into what would happen from an income tax perspective. I highly recommend that you hire a **Certified Public Accountant (CPA)** who can guide you according to your business goals and needs and take care of everything tax-related for you.

For example, upon analyzing your situation, a CPA can even set up a quarterly tax schedule, so you make smaller payments every three months, based on your estimated yearly income, instead of paying a big chunk in the beginning of the year.

The good news is that the money we pay CPAs for their hard work is tax-deductible, since it's a business expense. And there's no price tag on your peace of mind after knowing that it's all taken care of by a professional, so you can dedicate yourself to doing what you do best: translating or interpreting.

○ **Business Bills**

Talking about business expenses, let's brainstorm some of the bills you'll pay in order to keep your business running:

- **Physical Space** — You may have decided not to have a separate office outside your house to minimize your overhead. However, it doesn't mean that your home office comes for free. Whether you rent or own, a percentage of your rent or mortgage, based on the square footage of the room you dedicate to your work, is a business-deductible expense.

- **Electricity and Internet** — The utilities you need to run your business are also deductible and, like the physical space, you can calculate a percentage of your electricity and internet provider bills, so your business will be responsible for it.

- **Phone Line** — Whether you decide to have a dedicated landline or a separate cell phone for your business, your company will pay the bill. However, if you wish to avoid the extra expense and don't feel comfortable disclosing your personal number to clients, you can always order a unique number from Voice Over IP (VOIP) services and forward calls to your cell. That way, you can screen your calls better, because anything from that number will be business-related and you may choose to let it go to voice mail after business hours. Otherwise, you can also answer these calls directly on your computer with an appropriate headset, and even purchase affordable credits to make (VOIP) calls as well.

- **Computer and Peripherals** — As we talked about in the previous section, you may want to buy a more powerful computer or invest in a laptop. This purchase, as well as any other accessories you may need (from an ergonomic mouse and keyboard to a new monitor or printer) will also be a business expense.

- **Office Supplies** — Mostly paper, if you'll be printing out documents for your personal records. However, keep in mind that you can always save your important documents as PDFs (invoices, contracts, financial records, etc.) and back them up in external hard drives or in cloud systems, thus saving a few trees.

- **Membership Fees and Dues** — Inarguably, you'll enjoy great benefits, as well as learning and networking opportunities, once you belong to a professional association or organization—whether it is the American Translators Association (ATA) and one of its local chapters, or professional organizations that gather individuals working in a particular field of expertise that is your area of subject. Your membership fees and dues, as well as expenses related to participation in the events these groups organize, are also tax-deductible.

- **Subscription to Professional Publications** — If you need to stay up to date on what is going on in the T&I industry or your specialty field, subscriptions to trade magazines can be added to this list.

- **International Cable or Satellite TV** — If you live in a country where your source language is not mainstream, you may be able to deduct expenses related to getting access to international TV channels. That remains one of the best ways to consume the same kind of media (both news and entertainment) that native speakers are exposed to in your country of origin.

- **Health Insurance, Retirement Plans, and Life Insurance** — You may already be enjoying these and other benefits if you're working for a translation agency or the language department of a company. Maybe you're a part-time translator or interpreter with a formal employment elsewhere, or even be included in your spouse's plan. However, if you're doing it alone as a full-time language professional, or if your business will be the only income in your household, take a moment to think about all your options. You may be able to select insurance and retirement plans as an individual, taking a portion of your salary to pay for the respective premiums, or have your own company provide these benefits to you—which should then be tax deductible. There's also the option of paying for part of it yourself and having your company match these contributions.

✓ **REMEMBER: Run this list by your CPA to confirm which expenses apply to your case and the location where you live.**

Whether you're working as a freelancer or doing business as a company, there are some business procedures you must follow in order to get paid for your work.

Before you even translate the very first word to your client, you'll most likely need to sign some documents, which we've already mentioned above in **Legal Paperwork**. There are also a few steps we'll cover below in **Project Management**.

For now, let's focus on how to set your price, what payment methods you may request, and how to issue invoices and then collect payments.

o   **How to Calculate Your Rates**

Let me start out by saying that there is no magic formula to calculating how much you should charge for your work. There are so **many variables** that come into play that only you can sit down and weigh all of them to come up with a given number or range, depending on the variety of services you provide and your own circumstances.

One thing I can assure you is that knowing your **average output** will come in handy when calculating your rate. If you know you can translate X amount of words in a day's work and you think about your expenses and how much you need to earn in order to make a living, you could come up with a rate per word or per hour that you're comfortable with.

✓   **QUICK TIP: This doesn't mean you should charge a fortune if you can only translate 100 words per day... In that case, clients will most likely choose someone they consider more efficient and charge a more reasonable fee.**

Let's look at some of the variables you must consider when calculating your rate:

- **Average Output** — As mentioned above, if you know how many words you can translate in a given day, you'll be more prepared to plan a project accordingly and calculate the number of hours it will take you to complete it. The idea here is not to fall under the minimum wage in your location, so yours can be a sustainable operation that allows you to make a living.

- **Hours of Work** — You can't expect to put in a couple of hours of work every day and earn the same you would otherwise if you were working a "conventional" 9-to-5 job. If you decide to work as a translator or interpreter part-time, either because you'd like to contribute to the current household income or because you have another part-time job, your income should be consistent with said reality. If you're going to take the full-time plunge as a language professional, be realistic about it.

- **Type of Service** — Different tasks may be charged differently. In the T&I industry, you may provide the following services, among others:

  - Translating — written words
  - Interpreting — spoken words
  - Proofreading / Editing — revising someone else's work for language accuracy
  - Reviewing / Consulting — approving or rejecting language-related material for accuracy and cultural sensitivity
  - Localizing — translating / revising materials to adapt contents to the target market
  - Voice Narration — recording messages written / translated in your languages

- **Currency and Geography** — Here we will get into the age-old debate that people living in X country or charging in this or that currency are able to provide a lower quote than someone living somewhere else and charging in dollars or euros. You are the only one who truly knows your circumstances, and there will be disparities even inside the same country, since the cost of living in your city may be higher/lower than in a couple of towns over.

- **Language Combination** — Some language pairs will be cheaper or more expensive than others based solely on the concept of supply vs. demand. The languages known as FIGS (French, Italian, German, and Spanish) are mainstream and, consequently, there are more people offering services from/to them in combination with English, for example. However, if there is only a handful of translators in the world eligible to cover a rarer combination, odds are their prices will be higher.

- **Specialization** — Even within popular language pairs, some translators may be more familiarized with a specific area that only a few are able to address at a professional level. The more specialized one's knowledge is, the higher their fee will potentially be. We'll talk more about specialization in the next section.

> **Check the EXTRAS in this book for links to calculators that can help you find your rate range.**

Considering all the above, decide which unit of measure you're more comfortable with: **a per-word rate, a per-page price or a per-hour flat fee**. Keep in mind that most clients are comfortable paying per source word—that is, the amount of words contained in the original document—because it's a more quantifiable amount, especially if you're dealing with electronic documents that can be edited and whose word count is easily demonstrated by your word processor or CAT tool of choice.

However, there are certain documents and certain tasks that need to be charged differently, such as when you have a document that cannot be easily converted into a readable electronic format (i.e. a fax page, an image file, etc.) In some of these instances, your client may agree to make **payment based on the target word count**—that is, the total number of words of the translation itself, after the project is completed.

Lastly, you will also need to **consider whether you'll offer discounts while using a CAT tool**. You'll most likely be faced with this issue when working with translation agencies that demand CAT "A" or "B" while you work on their projects. It is a common practice in the industry, but you're the one who ultimately needs to consider it and make a decision based on your business setup.

In order to illustrate how CAT tool discounts usually work, let's use a very unrealistic rate per word as an example. Let's say you charge $10 per word (that would be great, wouldn't it?).

So, when you run a CAT tool report, the software will compare the current document to your database (also referred to as "Translation Memory," or "TM" for short.) Should it find sentences ("segments") that are identical or similar to what you've translated in the past, it will indicate the amount of **matches** that are 75-99% similar to your TM (which will then need to be adapted accordingly,) as well as the **100%** (exact) matches (which still need to be proofread so your previous translation matches the current context.) CATs can also identify **repetitions**, which are found in the document itself, (not your TM,) so basically once you translate that sentence the first time it appears on a document, your translation will be propagated through all repeated segments.

All other sentences that share no similarities with your previous work will be considered "**New Words**," that is, where the bulk of your efforts will be applied to during the translation.

Considering the rate on our example, you would then charge $10 per words that are considered "New," $7 per words that are considered "Matches," and $4 per words that are considered "Exact Matches" or "Repetitions."

Let's break it down one more time, so you can understand the concepts behind giving CAT discounts:

✓ **New Words — Segments in the current file that are completely unrelated to your Translation Memory.**

✓ **75-99% Matches — Segments that are somewhat similar to something you've translated in the past while using your CAT tool of choice and, consequently, were stored in your TM.**

✓ **100% Matches — Segments that are identical to something you've translated in the past while using your CAT tool of choice and, consequently, were stored in you TM.**

✓ **Repetitions — Segments that are not similar to what you translated in the past, but repeated throughout the document you're translating.**

Keep in mind that CAT tools don't do the work for you. You must "feed" your translations to it to populate a TM database that will be compared to the new material coming in. And, even though the same sentences were used in the past, it doesn't mean that the translation you decided to enter then will be appropriate now. In other words, your previous translations will work as suggestions to matches and repetitions, but you always make the final call. That means you still need to proofread your previous work to approve it and confirm that it is fitting to the current material.

Last, but not the least, you can always do your homework and visit websites, blogs, or personal profiles to check out what other translators working with your language combination and/or fields are currently charging. This should give you a good idea of where you stand as far as rates are concerned.

Also, remember you'll need to ultimately make a decision on **when to update your prices**. You'll decide the time frame, whether it is every couple of years or after a longer period of time. Translators are usually concerned when they need to have "the talk" with their current clients about raising their rates. However, if you have a solid relationship, have been working together for a few years and your client is happy with your services, they will have no problem with it because you're adding value to their business.

○   Payment Methods

I cannot emphasize enough how communication is important in this business. You must always talk to your client before assuming anything, so once your quote is accepted, make sure you check what payment options you can both agree on.

If you and your client are based in the same country, you can request a **check**, which is the best way to get paid if you don't mind weekly or monthly trips to the bank. Best of it all is that you don't have to pay any fees when making a deposit, so the total check amount goes right into your account.

However, if you work with clients in other countries, there may be a few bumps on the road that separates you from your payment. Of course you can ask them to send you a check, but it will most likely be in a foreign currency and you'll need to make sure your bank can convert it and deposit it to your account. If you work with a credit union, as opposed to a federal bank, chances are it will take you some time to finally get that payment cleared and there will be some fees involved in the process for running the check through a federal bank and converting the amount in a foreign currency.

If you come from another country and intend to address the translation needs of clients in that location, the easiest way to receive payment is to keep a **foreign bank account**. In order to do so, verify which demands your foreign bank makes, as far as the documents you need to produce and whether you can open an account even though you do not currently live in the country. You'll also need to ask whether the bank can receive checks directly and deposit them into your account. Otherwise, make sure you have a reliable friend or family member who's willing to take the occasional trip to the bank. And yet another thing you must keep in mind when having a bank account abroad is the tax law enforced by both the foreign country and the country where you now live, as far as bringing money back into your territory.

If keeping an account abroad is not an option, you can accept **wire transfers**. Make sure you talk to your bank manager first to learn more about the fees involved in this transaction. Odds are there is a flat fee that will be taken out of your payment both by your bank and by your client's bank. It can drastically reduce the amount that will finally be deposited to your account, so it may not be a good option for smaller invoices.

Once again, talk to your client to see if you can add that fee to your invoice, so the amount they owe you is not eaten up by bank fees. You should also make it clear that you do not wish that your client deduct their own bank fees from your payment, so you really receive the amount that reflects the work you've put into the project.

Now, if your client is in the United States and you're located somewhere else in the world, **Automated Clearing House (ACH)** may be the option for you. It would allow you to receive a direct debit transfer to a U.S. bank, which you can then transfer to a bank account in your country.

Another option to receive payment is using an electronic payment service. There are several companies entering the market as this alternative becomes more popular with more people buying products on line and more freelancers offering their services through the web.

One of the mainstream electronic transfer services you can explore is **PayPal**, which is by far the most popular e-payment solution available. It was started by eBay so people could make or receive payment for the products they bought or sold on the auction website.

PayPal allows you to accept e-payments from other PayPal users, but that doesn't mean your clients have to set up an accounts in order to pay you. It also processes payment cards, so they may use a **credit or debit card** to send you money.

You then have the option of transferring funds to your bank account, receiving a check from PayPal, or requesting a PayPal debit card that you can use to withdraw cash at ATMs or make payments wherever cards are accepted.

Among some great features offered by PayPal and other electronic payment sites is the fact that you can add a "Pay Now" button to your website, so clients know where to go to make e-payments to you. You can also create electronic invoices and email them to your clients when requesting an e-payment.

✓ **QUICK TIP: Make sure you do a background check to see whether the electronic payment services you've considered are really reliable. Ask other translators what their experiences have been and look for specific information on how they can protect your identity and account from fraud and scam techniques, also known as "phishing"—that is webpages or email messages that look legitimate, but are only intended to acquire your personal and financial information in order to withdraw funds from your account.**

However, be aware that convenience comes with a price tag. In order to stay in business, electronic payment sites charge a commission out of every payment you receive and these fees may be somewhat hard to calculate and anticipate because they highly depend on payment method, that is, whether your client sent you payment through their own account or used a credit/debit card. Another influencing factor is your client's geographic location and currency, as well as yours. And, keep in mind that the bigger the amount being transferred, the more these sites may deduct from the payment you received, so make sure you weigh all your options before choosing the payment method that is more cost-effective to you.

o   **Invoicing Practices**

As you should know by now, you must issue an invoice to your clients once you complete a project or a set of tasks. Keep in mind that it is your responsibility to collect payment, so don't leave it up to clients to remember when and how much they should be paying you.

The best way to issue invoices is sending it with the translated files as soon as the project is done, especially if you're dealing with a larger project and, consequently, a more substantial amount. However, some translators prefer sending invoices at the end of the month, so they can group small tasks together and collect a larger amount at once.

The key here is to **coordinate your payment dates**, according to your own needs and your client's terms. You don't want to wait longer than needed in order to get paid.

Most clients agree with "Net 30" paying terms, that is, they would make payment 30 calendar days after receiving your invoice. So, let's say you finished a small job on the 10th and waited until the 30th to issue the respective invoice; you would then be delaying your own payment, because it would be made by the end of the following month, not on the 10th, that is, a month after the file was delivered.

Nevertheless, if you're able to combine several tasks assigned to you by the same client into a single invoice, it may be worth waiting a little bit more for a larger payment.

Sometimes you'll come across those rare clients who have no problem making payment upon receiving an invoice or within just a few days. Others will agree on "Net 15," but some may also ask you to accept payment in "Net 45" or "Net 60."

On the other hand, some translation agencies may have a Work Request system already in place and they won't need a copy of your invoice to pay you correctly and on time. In any case, create an invoice the same way you would for other clients and keep it for your records.

And, when dealing with individuals, it is a good idea to **ask for advance payment**. Since regular people are obviously not companies used to having recurrent expenses with service providers, including translations and interpreters, it may become a little harder for you to collect payment from individuals AFTER the job is done and delivered.

Let's say your client is someone local, who needs personal documents translated. In that case, you can arrange a meeting in order to deliver the translation and request prompt payment on the spot.

However, if a client doesn't live close by, you can request advance payment by check, and only deliver the project once payment is cleared (just in case...)

Or, in order to expedite things, you can use an online service like PayPal to process electronic transfers or credit/debit card payments. Just keep the transaction fee in mind and make sure you add this cost to your final price.

✓ **REMEMBER: You are responsible for keeping your invoices in order and provide your client with the appropriate information, because there are only a few companies out there that are organized enough to keep track of how much they owe each one of their service providers.**

---

o   **Accounting Software Will Help You Stay Organized**

Let's talk a little bit more about invoices. As I said before, you can send a simple document or spreadsheet and that should be enough for any client. However, I strongly recommend that you convert it into PDF before you send it off to prevent anyone from tampering with it.

If you choose to use an accounting program, most of them have **invoicing capabilities**. That may be a smart business decision because this kind of software allows you to **enter your clients' information into a database** and then select them from a list when you're creating estimates and invoices for them. It really helps to keep your clients' data on a central location to speed up the process, and you may even **store information on your vendors**, that is, the colleagues you may eventually hire to work with you on a project.

Other information you can store in these programs include the services you offer, such as different language pairs, proofreading, language consulting, etc., as well as the respective rates charged per item.

Large-scale accounting software will also connect to your bank in a secure way for real-time updates on your balance, deposits and withdrawals.

Additionally these programs are able to run detailed reports—as long as the information was entered correctly in the first place—to save you lots of time and money during tax season. If you hire a CPA to take care of your taxes, they will really appreciate the organized information you provide them.

✓   **QUICK TIP: If you already have someone in mind you trust to manage your taxes, ask your CPA what accounting software is used at their offices, so you can install it to your computer and share your business file with them.**

○ **Collecting Late Payments**

After you've taken all proper measures to ensure payment (i.e. agreed on payment terms and submitted a timely invoice) there are a few things you can do if payment is late.

Once payment is one week overdue, **send your client a kind reminder** with another copy of the invoice that was previously issued, saying that your records show that payment should have been made on such and such date.

If you don't hear back from them within a couple of days, send out a second reminder and maybe write something like "**Second Attempt to Collect**" on the subject of the message.

If another few of days go by—and the invoice is now more than 15 days late—, you can go a step further and use **red bold font** to draw some attention to your email. That has worked in the past for me and some colleagues. People react rather strongly to red lettering (maybe it has something to do with memories of their school life) and usually reply right away with sincere apologies, followed by prompt payment.

Another tactic you may want to use with "repeat offenders" is to send them a letter explaining your **late fee policy**. Write a neutral, professional letter and create a table to indicate how much of a late fee would be applied to each 15 days a payment is late. Once clients do the math and see how much more they will have to pay you if they don't make proper arrangements, they will probably learn the lesson.

To sum it up, keep in mind that a professional-looking invoice will give your clients a good impression about your business and keeping a clear communication channel and good organization practices are the best ways to avoid any issues as far as getting paid. And, if your client puts all ethics aside and says that they will not be paying you for your services, you can always mention that you will

a) forward the case to a collection agency,
b) report their company to the authorities, and/or
c) share the experience on online forums dedicated to rating translation clients on their payment practices.

✓ REMEMBER: Being assertive, yet polite, will go a long way. Kindly remind your client that you provided a service, as any other professional would, and now there is a bill they must pay.

Explain that, as a practice in the translation industry, we can usually wait 15-30 days in order to get paid after the invoice is issued, while other bills they have are most likely paid at the moment services are provided.

If you feel comfortable, establish a comparison with doctors, lawyers, plumbers, etc. Point out how clients would hardly take the same approach—trying to delay payment—while shopping at the grocery store or paying their phone bill.

After all, you also need to go grocery shopping and pay your own bills, and that is exactly why you're collecting payment for the professional services you've provided...

Once again, be professional and confident, and always assess the situation before putting your "plan" into action. It all comes down to your previous agreement with your client and your personality, which will determine the approach you'll take when collecting payment.

Legitimate clients will appreciate your honesty and understanding, while scammers never intended to pay you in the first place.

(We'll talk more about scammers later...)

PROJECT MANAGEMENT

Let's now talk about **the flow of a typical translation project**, that is, all the steps you must anticipate from the time you receive a document that needs translation until it is finally delivered to your client. We'll also review some ideas on how to organize your projects, and bring in trusted colleagues to work with you when needed. Lastly, we'll discuss how to establish an **effective collaboration** with project managers who may send you projects from **translation agencies**.

o **Sending a Quote**

Once you have signed a Vendors Agreement, an NDA and an NCA, you'll receive a file that your client needs translated. After evaluating it in terms of language combination, target audience, field of specialization, level of difficulty and word count, you'll submit an estimate for your client's approval.

Your estimate may be anything from a simple email message indicating your price and delivery date and time, to something more elaborate using a document similar to your invoice template, which looks more professional. You can also attach word count reports from your CAT to substantiate your estimate, so clients know what they're paying for.

However, depending on the format of the file you receive, you'll have either an editable or a non-editable document. **Editable documents** are electronic files you can edit by adding your translation to it and removing the original content from it. Among them are text documents, spreadsheets, slide presentations, and publication files. If you can type and replace the original, it's an editable version.

On the other end of the spectrum, you'll have **non-editable documents**, considered to be hard-copy materials, that is, files you cannot add content to or remove anything from. They can be non-electronic files, as the old-fashioned paper documents sent out by regular mail or fax. That's easy to remember, because you'll have a physical copy of it in your hands—and that's a "hard copy."

But there are also non-editable electronic files, such as scanned documents usually saved as a JPEG or TIFF images or, most commonly, as a PDF, which stands for "Portable Document File"—and I'm sure it's something you're already familiar with.

If you receive editable electronic files, you can get a word count right away. But when you're working with hard-copy files, the issue that comes up is the fact that you cannot know right away how many words there are in the source material. You may feel like you're in the dark, with no idea on how much to charge for the project according to your per-word rate and how long you'll need to get it done, considering your average output.

If you're willing to make an investment, you can acquire a license for a document converter and try to extract the source text from it in order to have an editable file whose word count you can estimate.

These conversion programs are known as **Optical Character Readers** (OCRs) and they work with both non-editable electronic files you've received from your client by email, or physical documents you can scan into your computer.

> ✓ **QUICK TIP: One little note on this type of file conversion — If the original is in any language that uses accents and special characters, make sure the software supports languages other than English. Otherwise the result will be less than desirable because the program won't understand what those different letters mean and replace them with something else. For example, "ó" may be replaced with "6".**

So, unless you can effectively convert those hard-copy files into editable text, you'll need to work with "**guesstimates.**" In other words, you'll have to look at the contents and see what it "feels" right when it comes to charging for it and judging how fast you you'll be able to get it done. This is not an exact science, so odds are you may get a little frustrated when faced with your first projects of this nature until you feel more comfortable and confident in dealing with them.

What I mean is that this kind of "guesstimate" approach can backfire because, in the end, you may end up typing way more words than you expected and, consequently, work more hours than you estimated. If your "guesstimate" misses the mark, the math won't add up when you try to multiply that resulting word count by your per-word rate—your original quote could be well below that amount.

In such case, if your client is somewhat flexible, you can always let them know beforehand that you'll be **applying your per-word rate to the target word count**, that is, the amount of words in the final target document (i.e. your translation.)

If charging per target word count is absolutely out of the question—because your client demands to know exactly how much they'll be paying before the project starts—yet another approach you can take to make your "guesstimate" a little more accurate is to **count how many words there are in a typical line, how many lines there are in a typical page, and how many pages there are in the document**. In any case, it'll only give you a close approximation so you can be more comfortable with your total price and expected output, and you shouldn't miss the mark by all that much.

You may also need to invest more time than expected on translations originated by non-editable files if some "page formatting" is required to make the document look as closely as possible like the original. By the way, the name of this extra service is **Desktop Publishing** (or "DTP" for short) and translators should charge extra when working with non-editable files that need to mirror the original in their appearance.

Sometimes this task can be easily done in a word processor, especially if it only involves text style (bold, italics, underline, font color and size) and a few tables and graphic elements.

However, word processors have limited DTP capabilities and you'll most likely need to use publication software, which are programs used by advertising and publishing companies to design flyers, brochures, reports, newspapers, magazines, books, and any other type of professional-looking publications.

Additionally, in order to get a professional look, you'll need a whole different set of designing skills to make files look pretty. For better results, your client would need to provide you with all the **artwork**, that is, the graphic elements used in the original document. Do they have a logo and some pictures? Is there text within those pictures you need to translate as well? What color scheme did they use in the originals?

As you can imagine, DTP is a whole different animal to tame. So if you're not design-oriented, tell your client that you're strictly a language service provider and that another professional must be hired to take care of this task and have the final document ready to be published. Being honest and upfront will help you to avoid a lot of headaches later.

✓ **REMEMBER: Clients may not be able to read your translation and judge its quality, but they can get very upset if they look at the translation and it visually doesn't match the original.**

The best thing you can do in this case is to be on the same page with your client BEFORE you start working on a project. Do they only need the file translated and will they work with someone else to make it look like the original? Or do they expect you to translate AND format it as well?

If you're not comfortable formatting pages, you may need to hire a professional to take care of it, and their fee must be included in your estimate— otherwise, you're basically paying to work!

Before moving on with the preparation process, here's an idea on how to deal with text within images. Let's say you need to translate a brochure that you received as an editable file, but you noticed that some of the original text cannot be replaced with your translation because it is inside a picture—and images cannot be changed within a word processor or CAT tool.

You can't simply finish translating the editable content and send the file back to your client with those images still in the source language, even though it's not your fault that you don't have access to the text within those pictures in the first place.

In that case, it's best if you tell your client that you'll supply them with a **two-column file, with the source text you found within images on the left-hand side and your translation on the right-hand side**. That way, your client will be able to go back to the design team that created those pictures and have the appropriate target content inserted into it. And don't forget to add those extra words to your word count too, on top of the editable source text you've already translated.

✓ **QUICK TIP: When working on a two-column format, displaying side-by-side text for easy identification by monolingual DTP professionals, you can charge a typing fee for the source contents you typed and then your regular fee based on that word count for the translation you'll be providing.**

---

o   Receiving a Confirmation

Once you've taken all the items mentioned above into consideration in order to submit a quote, it'll hopefully be approved and you'll receive the green light to get the translation started. This confirmation will most likely come in the form of a **Project Number, Purchase Order (PO)** or **Work Order**

(WO)—any kind of reference you can use in your invoice in order to track the project you'll be working on.

Now you're finally closer to rolling up your sleeves and getting to work. There are just a few project management steps you still may need to take before you start working on the actual translation itself.

The file you received is referred to as the **source file**, since it is written in your source language, which is most likely your B or 2nd language. You are expected to send back the **target file** translated into your target language, which is most likely your A or 1st language.

So, a good practice before you type the first translated word is to click the option Save As in your program of choice to save a copy of the file and **add the target language code** at the end of the file name. That way, you'll keep the original source file intact while working on your translation. (You can skip this step if working with CATs, though.)

For example, let's say you've received a document called "Sales Contract.docx" in English and you need to translate it into Spanish. You then save it as "Sales Contract – ES.docx" and work on that copy, leaving the original as is for reference.

By the way, language-name standards may use two or three letters. For example, English can be either represented by "EN" or "ENG" and Spanish by "ES" or "SPA." If you've noticed, two-letter standards usually refer to the name of the language in its original ("ES" stands for "español") and three-letter standards refer to the name of the language as it is spelled in English ("SPA" stands for "Spanish.")

> **Check the EXTRAS in this book for a link to the ISO Language Code List.**

Another thing you must keep in mind for the sake of organization is how to **structure your folders and files**. One method that allows you to quickly retrieve your work at a later time is creating a folder with your client's name, which will then gather all projects worked on for that company or individual.

So, let's say you've received a project from Client A, to which you'll assign Invoice # 200, for example. Your client already told you that this project will include several files submitted throughout the next few weeks, so you'll need to create one folder for each file as it arrives at your inbox.

Here's what your folder structure would look like then:

- Client A
  - Invoice 200 – September 2014
    - 09-01 – EN-ES – 250 words
      - Announcement.docx
      - Announcement - ES.docx
    - 09-10 – EN-ES – 1,000 words
      - Webpage.docx
      - Webpage - ES.docx
    - 09-15 – EN-ES – 750 words
      - Product Launch.docx
      - Product Launch - ES.docx
    - 09-25 – EN-ES – 1,500 words
      - User Agreement.docx
      - User Agreement - ES.docx

As you can see, each task that is part of an invoice will be organized chronologically by **date, language pair, and word count**. This is the same information you'll list on your invoice, so it's better to keep everything simple and easy to correlate, just in case you need to refer to the material at a later time.

And, once everything is organized, you can finally start working on your translation, whether you'll be using a word processor or other software that allows you to edit the original, which could be a spreadsheet or slide presentation, or if you'll convert it into your CAT tool of choice in order to record your progress and feed your translation memory.

o **Delivering a Project**

Needless to say, once the translation is done, you must review it carefully while keeping the following in mind:

- Resolve any vocabulary decisions

- Compare source and target to eliminate mistranslations

- Correct typos, punctuation, or grammar errors

- Check if numbers were typed correctly and if units of measure were converted accurately (if applicable)

- Take care of the overall quality assurance and visual aspect of the document.

For your operation to really run even more smoothly, consider **teaming up with a proofreader** that can review your work and give you some feedback. You can then do the same with your colleague's translations, so both of you can include an added layer of quality assurance to your combined work.

Once everything is ready to go, you can finally deliver your translation, along with extra files your client may have requested:

- the final document in the target language

- a proofreading document showing correction marks and comments left by a reviewer, if you're working with a colleague as an extra set of eyes

- a glossary with the keywords used

- a bilingual file, if you used a CAT tool

- a translation memory, if you've agreed to create one

✓ **REMEMBER: When providing a TM along with your translation, make sure that you either export the contents of the document you just worked on, or create a database dedicated to that client in particular, so as not to share proprietary information from other clients.**

This is something that may happen if you create a translation memory dedicated to a language combination or a field of expertise and feed it with projects from all your clients without making a distinction of what contents belong to whom.

Sharing information from your clients to third parties is, to say the least, unethical. And, if you've signed an NDA, it's a severe breach of contract.

o   Working With Colleagues

Since we talked about teaming up with a colleague to act as your proofreader, let's explore the idea of having a translation team. **The best way to find someone you can trust and who can benefit from your help is networking.**

Maybe you've taken a class or training program, attended a conference or seminar, or joined professional groups on internet forums or social media websites. These are all good options to start interacting with potential colleagues who may complement or add value to your services. Watch how they behave in person and online, learn about their experiences and areas of specialization, pay attention to the tips they share and the questions they ask.

Teaming up with other translators will only help you grow and achieve your goals:

- Increase output when working as a pair of translators

- Oversight and added quality assurance—because two minds think better than one

- Diversification in fields of specialization

- Diversification in language combination

- More localization options—applicable to languages spoken in several countries, with "regional flavors"

- More availability if you're in different time zones

Check SECTION 3 to read more about networking and interacting with client and colleagues.

When working with colleagues, make sure you agree on their rate and pay them accordingly. **The one thing you could do to burn bridges quickly is not treating colleagues with the same respect you wish to be treated.** For example, do not delay payment on services your colleagues have provided to you just because you're still awaiting payment from your client. Plan ahead and honor your commitment to your colleagues, no matter what your arrangements with your own client may be.

o   **Working With Project Managers**

Project Managers, or PMs, are like the salespeople of a company, but instead of selling a product to a customer, they are the middle-people who assign translation projects from big corporations to language service providers.

PMs are mostly employed by large translation agencies, but your contacts could also work for the language department of a corporation. They may take care of a couple of language combinations that are relevant to their employer or be in charge of a specific segment within the company and need product brochures, financial statements, or website material translated.

Even if you haven't worked with PMs before, you probably have a pretty good idea of how things should go. They receive projects from end clients, assign them to a suitable translator like you, and act as the facilitator for both payment matters and questions or concerns you may have.

If you find good language companies and PMs, that's great! They should be the majority of the cases out there—and that's the expected scenario. However, we're gonna talk about the dark side, the worst-case scenarios, so you're prepared to act when a similar negative situation comes along.

PMs may try all tricks in the book to have you go their way. They'll say **it's a small project**, so there must be a way for you fit it into your schedule and send it back quickly, without applying any "rush rate" because it is indeed really, really small. Or they'll say that **the project is too easy**—as if they were translators themselves and could make that judgment—so of course **you'd see no problem charging only half your regular rate, right?**

I hope it never happens to you, but if you do meet a difficult or unrealistic PM, you'll need to stand your ground. Know your price and output and don't be afraid to say no. You're a professional and shouldn't be pushed around. Besides, you don't wanna be stuck with a badly-paying assignment when your dream project comes along.

You'll realize sometimes that the email a PM sent out about an upcoming project was actually a general message, and not really directed at you. What happens is that PMs usually have access to an internal database at their agency that was generated when translators submit a copy of their resume, or which may even get updated every time translators visit the agency's website and create an account to fill in a profile themselves. And, **unfortunately, many PMs will resort to mass emails** in order to get anyone to work on a project, so they can move on to the next item on their list. **And that's when getting a project assigned to you becomes more like an auction: the lowest bidder takes it all!**

Good PMs will work responsibly and try to match a translator's experience and background to the needs of their end clients. Bad PMs will act irresponsibly and go for whoever charges the least and promises to deliver it faster, so they can maximize their commissions and company profits.

Good translation agencies will pay their translators according to the terms they had previously agreed on, regardless of their arrangements with the end client. **Promising a discount to end clients, whichever the reasons may be, does not make it mandatory for translators to accept a lower rate.** Additionally, bad translation agencies will use excuses and delay payment to translators if anything went wrong with the payment they should have received from the end client, which is yet another example of poor project management practices.

Likewise, **taking a huge translation project and distributing little bits and pieces to a large group of translators is not an ideal practice.** Let's say there's a 100-thousand-word manual and 10 translators were hired to work on it. Because the project is being managed by a translation agency, most likely these translators are working isolated from one another and cannot exchange ideas on how they're going about their respective pages and sections.

Then, after the translation is done, the PM only has to put it all together and send it back to the client. At first, the client will be happy to get a 100-thousand-word job done in about a week, but if the translation is into a language they don't understand, how are they supposed to know if the final product truly reflects the quality they expected?

There's nothing wrong in dividing a large project among several translators to expedite the process. However, it is crucial to either have them work together, as a cohesive team that will strive to have a consistent vocabulary throughout the document, or hire an editor who can make sure the translation "speaks" in one single voice after the work is done.

You can probably imagine the implications of an inconsistent translation. If a manual was translated by several people and they didn't use the same term for a part or component, **the outcome will be confusing**, to say the least. If we're talking about a manual for a toy or household appliance, it may lead to frustration on the part of the consumer; but if we're taking about a medical device or a piece of equipment used by construction workers, for example, **consequences may be fatal**.

In this worst-case scenario, there are a few parties to be blamed. On a higher level, **the language company is not doing its job when their only goal is save time and money**, because they'll most likely compromise on quality and consistency. On a middle level, **the end client isn't asking the right questions** to assure that it will have the professional quality they expect; after all, this translation will probably represent their products or services before consumers in a foreign market.

And, on the lowest level, **translators** are also to blame when they knowingly accept a project like that. Even though they may do the best possible job they can, they are **contributing to the illusion that large projects can be done effectively overnight**.

As translators, when you come across someone on a job board who's willing to work for a fraction of what you intend to charge, there's really little you can do about it. But upon participating in project that is set up like this, you do become part of the problem. The best you can do is say "no" and educate your client.

PMs often don't appreciate this kind of talk and they'll look somewhere else to do things their way. If that's what it takes, let it be. Burning bridges is never a good idea, but neither it is to work on a project that will have negative consequences for the target audience, that is, the people who will actually benefit from the product of your work.

In the example we've been using about the translation of a manual, the target audience could be a child using that toy, someone using an electronic gadget or household appliance, doctors and nurses using a medical device to save a life, or a construction worker operating a piece of equipment and putting his life on the line.

Keep in mind that sometimes it feels good to say "no" to a project when you know you can't make it for professional or personal reasons. Besides, saying "no" may not even be equal to burning bridges at all. The way some agencies work, you'll most likely receive a message a couple of days later from another PM or even the same PM with more potential project requests. So **know when to pick your battles and stick to your principles.**

o   **Crowdsourcing**

Yet another topic we should explore on this same subject is "crowdsourcing." If you've never heard of this method, it's a common practice nowadays **when companies turn to people who aren't in their payroll to try and solve an issue, instead of using their own human resources or hiring advisors**.

In other words, these companies "outsource work to the crowd," and the help they seek is usually for free, or in exchange of some sort of perks (i.e. recognition, social status, badges identifying the people involved as project collaborators, etc.) and it can cover a wide variety of bases. Most of the times, it's connected to marketing efforts, so they can make better decisions when trying to appeal to their consumers.

When applied to translations, "crowdsourcing" means to gather a large group of people—whether they are professionals, bilingual individuals without any background in translation, or simply language learners—to work on the same piece for free or for any item other than actual payment for their time.

One famous example was the attempt that **LinkedIn** made when they looked for translators who had created a profile on their professional network, and tried to get their website translated for free in exchange of credit, a premium account, or other inside deals. The effort backfired and LinkedIn received a letter from the **American Translators Association (ATA)**, besides some angry messages from the translators who were contacted themselves.

On the other hand, **Facebook** successfully had their website translated by combining community input and the oversight of professional translators. In order to do that, they implemented a system in which users from different backgrounds could contribute to the site localization effort with translations into their native language, then rate suggestions made by their peers, while the translators who were effectively hired by the website translate and approve the final version that goes live.

As you can see, "crowdsourcing" can be a good idea, but it can contribute to the very same issue we just discussed, that is, when PMs divide a large job into little pieces and distribute it to several people without any checks and balances.

And, when the client doesn't know any better because they don't speak the target language, end users may suffer and our entire professional category doesn't get the credit it deserves, because **translation ends up being seen as something easily done by the push of a button.**

✓ **REMEMBER: Everything we do as a translator represents our whole professional category, so we do have the power to make things better in such a competitive, yet growing industry through client education and awareness. There is room for everyone, especially considering the amount of information generated every day that needs to be translated to other languages, so there is no need to cannibalize the system in exchange of perks or a couple of cents.**

---

o **Editing, Proofreading, Back Translation and Reviewing**

Different clients have their own idea of what each one of these concepts mean, so make sure that you're on the same page before you start working on a request that involves **editing, proofreading, or reviewing**. For some clients, any of these requests may mean **checking a translation performed by someone else**. If that is the case, give it a once over before you send out a quote. The quality of the material may range from pretty good to unintelligible—to the point that it's better to just start it all over again.

What happens in some cases is that clients may have asked someone who is not a professional (i.e. their secretary, their nephew who took the source/target language at school, etc.) to work on a document and, unsure of the final quality, decides to hire a language service provider to "polish it up." Worst-case scenario, a document was put through a machine and now you need to make sense of what was spit out on the other end... By the way, that's known as **post-editing machine translations**.

If you'll be only fixing some minor mistakes, such as spelling and grammar, or maybe improving the flow of a few sentences to make them sound more natural, you could charge about half to three quarters of your translation rate. However, if the material is of a very, very poor quality, be honest with the client. Otherwise, you may realize that it's more trouble than it's worth.

Be also prepared to receive **back-translation requests**, which is yet another concept you must check with your client beforehand. Some clients expect you to **translate a translation back into the source language** by using a "word-for-word" approach, so they can check whether the original translator was accurate. Other clients will expect you to render a readable version back in the original language, that is, not word-for-word.

Ultimately, we also have **review requests** that concern your own translation. When it happens, you must be prepared to stand by the decisions you made in your translation, just as much as you'll need to admit when you made a mistake and correct it accordingly.

When editors make changes to your file in a way that you can actually see exactly what was changed, the process is relatively easier. Most often, this is done using the **Track Changes** function in Microsoft Word, **Edit Changes** in Open Office or Libre Office, or balloons with **comments** added to a PDF. In other cases, the editor may have **highlighted** what they changed or used a **different font color** to make it stand out. In either case, check each change and make a decision on whether to accept the correction or offer an explanation on why you believe you made the right decision in the first place.

Unfortunately, clients aren't always worried about making it easier for translators and you may receive edited files without any indication of what was actually changed. Once in that situation, take a deep breath and open the reviewed file and your original translation side by side. If you use Microsoft Office, you can use the **Review > Compare** option and the program will analyze both versions and tell you what was changed.

When presenting a review report back to the client, you'll need to **either concede your point or defend your opinion** and back it up with trustworthy sources. Simply saying, "that's the way it is in my language" won't be good enough, so try to find articles from reputable authors or organizations that use the same terminology, or look up the words and expressions in question to present your client with definitions and examples that support your work. Also, always refer to a good grammar book in case grammar mistakes have been pointed out.

✓ **In very special cases, clients will tell you that your word choice is wrong and, even if you make a strong point to indicate otherwise, there's nothing you can do but make the proposed change to accommodate their preferences—after making a brief disclaimer that you do not agree with it. After all, the client is always right... right?**

You'll need to make this review process as clear and as professional as possible. **Don't take anything personally** and remain open-minded, friendly, and honest. Ask yourself what kind of corrections you could find: **Grammar? Vocabulary? Spelling? Style? Register?** Use the initials G, V, Sp, St, and R to mark your comments on why you think the client decided to make changes to your translation, providing a legend so the PM or client's editor can follow your thinking process.

One suggestion is to create a blank document, changing the page orientation to "Landscape", so you have more room to lay out your comments and explanations. Start by creating a five-column table and use the 1st column to paste the original sentence in the source language, so you'll always have a starting point for your comparison. Then, in the 2nd column, paste the translation you provided to that sentence in the target language. The 3rd column would be dedicated to the correction made by the client's editor and the 4th column will provide a neutral explanation.

Don't talk about what you think or feel; provide carefully chosen links to support your case, so make sure they are written by native speakers and error-free. After all, you're looking for an independent authority in the target language that will back you up. This is also the best place to paste dictionary definitions, always pointing out where the information came from. And, in the event that an editor's correction was spot on, thank them for the input and accept the change gracefully.

The 5th and last column is where you make your final judgment and offer your recommendations. You may suggest that the client keep your original translation or point out that the revised version should be used. You can also combine your sentence and their sentence to make an even better target sentence that has best of both worlds.

Following is an example of what your reviewing table would look like. This is also a good template you can use if you are hired to act as a text editor and review somebody else's work.

Source Sentence	Target Sentence	Editor's Version	Explanation	Final Suggestion
¡Estoy embarazada!	I'm pregnant!	I'm embar-rassed!	Embarazada = esperando un hijo (expecting a child) Embarazada. com	I'm pregnant!
Don't pretend!	¡No pretendas!	¡No finjas!	Pretender = tener la intención (intend to) RAE **Thanks for catching that!**	¡No finjas!

Lastly, when reviewing your own work after it's been through an editor, use your best judgment to decide whether you'll charge for it. If the editor actually improved upon your work, you should not charge anything additional to your original translation rate.

However, clients may come to you and express their confusion when they see that your translation went through substantial changes. If your client doesn't speak the target language and editors didn't do their job properly by either (a) worsening the quality of your translation when introducing errors due to lack of knowledge or (b) pointing out synonyms and making style changes just to show they were doing their job, this kind of review request will demand even more of your time to disprove that most corrections are inaccurate or unnecessary. If that is the case, let the client know that you'll be charging an hourly rate in order to provide a review report.

SELL YOUR PROFESSIONAL SERVICES

The T&I industry is **very competitive** precisely due to the perks that draw many people to it in the first place: mobility, flexibility, and ownership of your income and schedule. People all over the world are trying to get the attention of potential clients and maybe strike a long-term collaboration deal. But, don't worry; I'm not trying to discourage you from pursuing a career in the field. I do believe **there's room for everybody, because every translator is unique** and persistence really pays off when you're trying to find your place in the sun.

The best way to stand out from the crowd is to find your **specialization** and target your services to the correct audience—especially if you work with a very popular language pair. And, in order to do just that, in this section we'll talk about finding your niche, seeking continued education, building your online presence, offering diversified services, and exploring different networking opportunities.

More specifically, we will discuss how to put together a **translation-specific resume**, write **cover letter** templates, create professional **profiles**, apply for translation projects through **job boards**, and use **social media** to your advantage.

If you're yet to start working in the field, or you're looking forward to expanding your business, the fact that you're taking the time to educate yourself already indicates you're in the right direction. This is the right time to work hard on your **marketing strategies**, so you don't put all your eggs in one basket. It's easier to have everything ready to go now, and then do some weekly or monthly maintenance, instead of balancing the launch of your career from the ground up while you already have translation projects in progress and deadlines to meet.

In other words, if you wait until you're a well-established professional before you start promoting your services, you most likely will not be able to create a sustainable business. **The idea is to get everything in gear before you get started.**

SPECIALIZATION AND CONTINUED EDUCATION

After reading *Section 1* of this book, you got to know yourself better as a translator, at least from a more technical perspective (current skills, researching abilities, what needs to be improved, how to stay organized, your average output, etc.). Now, you should ask yourself **what you would really be good at** when acting as a translator or an interpreter and work towards **improving your knowledge.**

o   **Find Your Competitive Edge**
The first thing you might want to do is to find your specialty, your niche, your competitive edge. If you're **already familiar with a specific field**, you will probably work more efficiently when you're translating and interpreting subjects related to that area in particular.

Do a brainstorming session to consider your **professional background**, as well as your **hobbies** and **interests.** Maybe you majored in Biology and could do a great job in life sciences and environmental translations. Or you used to work at a school and became familiar with documents like certificates, transcripts, consent forms, and information on SATs and state regulations, so Education may be a great field for you. And, in your spare time, you may enjoy running or cooking, so you probably have a lot of knowledge in these two areas that you could put to good use as a translator of articles or books about these subjects.

As mentioned before, what will take you from being one among many "Language A to Language B" translators is your **specialization**, that something extra you have to offer. Your main field(s) will put you ahead of the competition and make you stand out. After all, clients will be more inclined to hire former engineers who have become translators, for example, instead of translators of general subjects who would like to try their hand at engineering projects.

> ✓ TRUE STORY: A client on a job board needed some product specifications translated from Portuguese to English. The subject? Manufacturing baby bottles and pacifiers. I applied for it and was awarded the project after I mentioned that my daughter had just turned one. The client figured that I knew a thing or two about the subject to do a good job. Through my personal experiences, I had instinctively acquired knowledge on BPA, nipple sizes, and heating devices, and I was able to put it to practice during the translation project. Of course having a baby is not classified as a "hobby" or "special interest," but it qualified me to do a professional job, even though I hadn't had any hands-on translation experience in my resume related to this specific subject... until then.

Once again, your language combination may seem overcrowded, but if you find your specialization and play your cards well, you can stand out as a member of a select group of experts in a given area, the go-to person when clients need Language A to Language B in a particular XYZ field.

Do your best to go against the current trend of **becoming a generalist**, that is, someone who claims to translate absolutely anything. This *is* **largely a myth**, by the way, because certain areas require specialized knowledge and anything else, despite the best of intentions and the hardest of efforts, will always fall short of the ideal.

At first, your natural instinct may be to accept any offers coming your way, but being honest will take you a long way and clients appreciate it if you say "no" and explain why you are unable to provide a particular service to them. In order to assure a long-lasting career as a translator or interpreter, **know your limitations and be true to yourself.**

○　Never Stop Learning

The good news is that, once you find your specialization, you'll know how to market your services to the correct crowd. The even BETTER news is that, once you establish yourself as a translator, you never stop learning.

Experts aren't the ones who know everything about their field of expertise; **experts are those who continue to improve their knowledge** in their subjects of interest, so that they can be on top of new developments in related technology.

When you stop to think about it, it really makes sense, doesn't it? There is no area of knowledge that will reach a point at which no possible developments could ever take place. With that in mind, you must seek **continuing education** in your areas, not only as a way to stay informed of new processes, procedures, and discoveries, but also to improve your vocabulary in your working languages.

Passive learning is something that actually works to the benefit of all of us translators. You may be **having a conversation with someone, listening to a radio show, watching something on the TV, reading a newspaper, magazine or a book** and acquiring more knowledge about your area, as well as at the linguistic level. Then, when you put your translator hat back on, you'll be able to recall that information that has been stored in the back of your mind—make notes you can use as a cheat sheet later on, if you must.

When it comes to **active learning**, look not only for translation-specific **webinars, conferences, and classes**, but also learning programs that don't deal directly with language skills and are aimed at presenting the subject matter to professionals working in the field.

Here's a concrete example: let's say you specialize in EH&S (Environment, Health & Safety) in a corporate setting, which means that you work on a regular basis with training materials that will be used by employees who must stay healthy, work safely, and avoid the negative environmental impact their activities may have. You can research vocabulary-related material to become familiar with keywords, but that may not be enough. Look for sessions you can attend and that talk about different aspects of EH&S, such as PPEs (Personal Protective Equipment) or CSR (Corporate Social Responsibility.) If possible, schedule a visit to a manufacturing plant and have someone walk you through the facilities, so you can see in real life what it is like to work with the tools described in the training program, or visit a neighboring community where social and cultural projects are being developed to improve the quality of life of people working in those facilities.

Another great way to learn more about your area of interest is to seek **volunteering** opportunities. You may not be able to be assigned a translation project right away due to lack of experience in a given field, but if you volunteer your time to an organization that promotes a cause that is close to your heart, odds are you'll acquire a diversified knowledge in the area and, on top of that, be able to "beef up" your resume with that learning experience.

These are only some ideas on how you can seek specialized knowledge in a field, that is, by **going where the end users of your work live and breathe**. But, yet another effective way to solidify knowledge is to prepare materials yourself.

Have you ever found yourself understanding something more clearly once you explain it to someone else? Well, if you're an expert in a given subject, **share your knowledge**! It will not only help you feel more comfortable as a technical writer or presenter, but also **highlight you as an authority** in the subject, and **contribute to your marketing efforts**.

We'll talk more about marketing ideas in the next few pages, but now is a good time to do another brainstorm session and jolt down ideas on **presentations** you could make or **articles** you could publish about your specialization.

TARGETED RESUME AND COVER LETTERS

Have I mentioned this is a **very fast-paced industry**? As we saw in *Section 1*, being effective and able to deliver projects on time is no longer a competitive edge, but a necessity. Now we'll talk about yet another component related to speed: summarizing your experiences in a **resume that is tailored to the T&I industry** and creating **cover letter templates** that you can personalize according to the project or client you're targeting.

"How is that related to speed?" you might ask. Well, it will definitely **streamline the project-quoting process**, so you don't have to reinvent the wheel each time you apply for a project. And, on the other hand, a **well-structured resume or cover letter** will also allow potential clients to skim through your information and find everything they're looking for in order to make a quick decision whether you hire your services.

○ **A Resume That Appeals to the T&I Industry**

Let's start with the basics: the resume. You should really do your best to **keep it short**—to match the attention span of many Project Managers out there, who must make a decision within a few seconds whether they will hire you or not.

Yes, it is possible to have a one-page resume and still highlight your most relevant translation accomplishments. And, while there really is no right or wrong in resume building, you should avoid making it long, cluttered, and complicated. Remember that PMs unfortunately won't have time to read about your objectives, list of workshops you've attended, or where you went to elementary school and high school.

A **clean and concise** resume should have your **personal information** at the top, including name, address, phone and fax numbers, email addresses, website, and instant message user names. Most importantly, NEVER forget to mention your **language pairs**.

> ✓ QUICK TIP: One of the worst things you can do in your resume is actually burying such an important piece of information, YOUR LANGUAGE PAIRS, somewhere else on the page or, worse, not even mentioning it at all. Your name and language pair should be one of the first things your potential clients see when they pick up your resume.

You can then list your **fields of specialization**. If you majored in a given area, let's say Business Administration, it should naturally be your specialization because you most likely have a lot more knowledge in that area than the average person. *(See the topic about Specialization above.)*

Your current professional career is also your field of specialization. If you are an administrative assistant at a doctor's office, for example, who could better translate medical records or informational flyers about medical services? If you dedicate yourself to an activity or a hobby, you could potentially become a very good professional translator in that area, too. If you are a wine connoisseur and have been to wine-tasting venues countrywide—or even worldwide—you could tackle some enology assignments.

The next section of your resume could be dedicated to your **professional experience**. List the starting and end month and year when you held a position, the name of the organization, location (city, state, country) and a very brief explanation of your duties and responsibilities.

If you have hands-on experiences in the T&I industry, list your **most relevant projects** in the next section. Mention the month and year when you completed these projects, the language pair, and some general info about it. Keep in mind that you'll probably be editing this section very often, because the idea isn't to list EVERY single translation project you completed in your life, but the more prominent ones that truly showcase your diversity and flexibility as far as content is concerned.

> ✓ **REMEMBER:** Ask your client's permission to use their company/product name. If you signed an NDA, odds are you can't disclose such info, but if you submit exactly what you intend to write to their approval, they may say yes. Otherwise, disclose only general information, such as the nature of the project and the areas to which they were related.

No translation experience? No problem! Consider **volunteering** opportunities that show you are so passionate about the industry that you actually make time to donate your services as a translator or interpreter to a cause that matters to you. *(See the topic about Specialization above.)*

At the bottom of your resume, you can list your **educational background**. List your Associate's, Bachelor's or Master's Degree, PhD, or professional certificate—in other words, your professional degrees and/or certificates. Next to your title, you can mention the beginning and end years you spent studying that subject, as well as the school and location.

If you have room, mention technical information, such as your **computer and internet specifications** and the **CAT tools** you use. It's a good idea to also list the **professional associations** you belong to—be them related to translating and interpreting or other career and activities—as well as any instances when you were a **keynote speaker** at an event.

Still some room left? Why not mention your **hobbies and interests**? As explained earlier, that may also qualify you to translate the subjects you're knowledgeable about.

As an example, you can find a copy of my resume on the following page.

RAFA LOMBARDINO, CT
(EN/PT, EN/ES)

translations@wordawareness.com
http://www.wordawareness.com
T: 858-200-5844 | F: 866-896-6120 | California, USA

LANGUAGE PAIRS

English > Portuguese / Portuguese > English (Certified by the American Translators Association, 2007 & 2013)
Spanish > English / English > Spanish (Professional Certificate, UC San Diego Extension, 2005-2008)
Spanish > Portuguese, Italian > Portuguese, Italian into English (additional languages since 2002)

MAIN FIELDS

Computers and Technology, Communications, Business and Human Resources, Education, Foods & Beverages, Cosmetics, Chemicals, EHS (Environment, Health and Safety), Legal

PROFESSIONAL EXPERIENCE

01/2010 – Present:	University of California, San Diego Extension – Translation Instructor
07/2009 – Present:	Word Awareness, Inc. – Director
05/2004 – 07/2009:	RML Language Services – Director
11/2004 – 03/2005:	JobSummit.com, text editor and lead generator for online job board. Occasional projects included data processing and creating spreadsheets
02/2003 – 12/2003:	Brazilian Pacific Times, text editor, page designer, photographer, reporter, and printing technician for a bilingual 36-page monthly tabloid targeted at the Brazilian community living in California
02/2001 – 10/2002:	Freelance English and Computer instructor for senior citizens.
02/2000 – 12/2000:	NESE (Social and Economical Studies Center) data processor and researcher for studies concerning unemployment rates and consumer behavior, which were supervised by the School of Business Administration at Universidade Santa Cecilia in Brazil
02/1998 – 12/2000:	Johnny-on-the-Spot English School, ESL instructor for groups of children (5-12 year olds) and teenagers, as well as individual classes for adults.
07/1997 – 07/2004:	Freelance translator

MOST RELEVANT PROJECTS

08/2010 – Present:	EN>PT	Training material for Dell Sales Representatives
04/2008 – 12/2009:	EN, PT, ES	News articles for InfoSurHoy.com, a news site about Latin America
06/2007 – Present:	EN, PT, ES	Employee survey, reports, and letters for Universal Technology Corp.
11/2005 – Present:	EN, PT, ES	Contracts, news clippings, MSDSs, product brochures, employee training, letters, and EHS & CSR reports for The Dow Chemical Company
06/2005 – Present:	EN, PT	Website localization, product brochures, restaurant menus, and distributor agreements for direct-sales company Tahitian Noni International, which makes healthy drinks and personal care products
11/2005 – 02/2008:	EN > PT	Military magazine for the US South Command
07/2005 – 07/2006:	EN > PT	Website localization, product brochures, and agreement for computer hardware manufacturer Maxtor
03/2004 – 06/2004:	PT > EN	Legal and business documents (tax receipts, contracts, agreements, legal statements from attorneys, and judicial decisions) about a Brazilian company that would be acquired by a U.S. corporation
10/2000 – 04/2001:	EN > PT	News articles about technology, culture, and politics for the on-line Brazilian version of Wired News, a U.S. technology magazine

OTHER PROJECTS

Personal documents, such as birth and marriage certificates, school transcripts, diplomas, letters, police records, provision of service contracts, and marketing brochures for individuals and small businesses.

VOLUNTEER WORK

Articles about women's rights; articles about Cystic Fibrosis; manuals and help files for open-source software; interviews with Chilean and Brazilian musicians for a documentary

EDUCATION

Bachelor's Degree in Social Communications, Major in Journalism (1999-2002):
Higher Education Institution, Universidade Santa Cecilia – Santos, São Paulo – Brazil
Associate's Degree in Computer Sciences, Emphasis on Data Processing (1995-1997):
Technical High School, Colégio Liceu Santista – Santos, São Paulo – Brazil

CAT TOOLS

Swordfish (compatible w/ Trados, Wordfast & SDLX, software for which I also have full licenses)

PROFESSIONAL ASSOCIATIONS

American Translators Association (ATA), Portuguese, Spanish, Italian and Company Division Chapters – Member
Association of Translators and Interpreters in the San Diego Area (ATISDA) – Founding Member

As you will see, I was able to fit everything in one page. Of course many items were left out, but I always keep a separate list of relevant projects to give clients details about my professional background if a theme in particular comes up during email exchanges or a meeting.

Keep in mind that your resume is supposed to be an abstract of your work history, not a novel about your ups and downs as a professional. The person on the other end of the screen or holding a paper copy of your resume will be pressed for time and only glance at your information, at first, in order to label you within seconds, so they can make quick a decision. Later on, they may go back and take a more in-depth look, but **potential clients should NEVER be digging for the information—it should jump right out of the page.**

✓ **QUICK TIP: You can always use your professional website or profiles on translation-related job boards to feature all extra information that didn't fit in the resume.**

Still on the subject of resumes, there is a big debate on whether you should use your **picture** and provide **personal information**, such as date of birth, marital status, how many children you have, and political or religious beliefs.

I say it's a big debate because it's closely related to cultural background. In general, European and Latin American clients are more open to getting this personal information beforehand. After all, it tells them who you are and may help them to make a decision whether to assign a project to you.

However, American clients won't feel very comfortable with TMI ("too much information") about you and are afraid you may believe you were turned down due to discrimination, considering the U.S. Equal Employment Opportunity initiative.

If clients wish to get to know you better, they may do so later on, after you establish a professional relationship, while exchanging messages with you during assignments or by sending you an invitation to some of the several social networking websites out there. The thing is that there will be time to socialize with your clients if and when they make the first move. Great friendships can develop from what started as a business deal, and that makes our field even more exciting and fun. Still, most clients expect a strictly-professional relationship and will feel uncomfortable if you offer too much personal information, so watch for cues and develop your relationship accordingly.

Considering this, if you intend to find clients worldwide it's best that you keep a neutral resume that highlights you as a professional. On the other hand, there's nothing wrong with having different versions of your resume. You can write it in each of your working languages to target clients who can't read your A or B language, or craft your projects and experiences according to your specializations.

For example, I have the general, technical resume I shared above, but I also have a literary-focused resume that I send to publishers and authors I would like to work with.

✓ **QUICK TIP: When replying to a request for resumes posted at a job board, for example, check where your potential client is located and whether they mention anything about resume formatting, so you can match their expectations. For example, some European clients are adamant about receiving resumes that follow the Europass instructions and template, which means that anything different from what they expected will be ignored.**

One more thing about creating a resume: I highly recommend that you convert it into a PDF, so the file doesn't get too "heavy" to be sent by email and the contents don't "shift" on the page depending on the program that clients use to open your document. Lastly, if you send a PDF version, your information cannot be edited that easily—there's always a way when ill-intentioned people want to do something wrong, unfortunately. But that's a subject for another topic you'll find under *Leave Your Mark Online* further down in this section.

o **Cover Letter Templates**

Keep in mind all of the recommendations above when creating your cover letters as well, because it will be the best way for you to communicate with clients on line. Be equally clear and to the point, so project managers can scan through it and check whether they identify the information they're looking for.

You can use cover letters when **applying for a translation project** if a company or translation agency has already posted an announcement on a job board or translation forum, or when **introducing yourself to a potential client**.

As a matter of fact, it's best if you create several cover letter templates to save time and effort. Let's say your main fields are medical, marketing, and human resources and that you work with English-to-Spanish and French-to-Spanish translations. You could then create several cover letters for each combination and field. English-to-Spanish medical reports? French-to-Spanish marketing analysis? HR paperwork both in English and French to be translated to Spanish? Each letter would only have information specific to a language or field to help your potential clients make an informed decision on why you're the best match for their project.

You'll find an example of a cover letter template on the following page, but as a general suggestion, you should open it up with an **introduction**, mentioning your name and language pair and how you came across your potential client's information. Was it a job board? Their company website? A friend who works for that organization who told you they may be looking for a translator?

Dear Mr./Ms. [INSERT POTENTIAL CLIENT'S CONTACT NAME]

This is Rafa Lombardino, Project Director at Word Awareness, Inc., a small network of translators who have been individually providing translations into their native languages for at least five years. We have just received a message regarding your post at [INSERT SOURCE NAME] and would like to collaborate with [INSERT POTENTIAL CLIENT'S COMPANY NAME] in future assignments involving [INSERT LANGUAGE PAIR AND/OR FIELD].

[INSERT TRANSLATOR'S INFO]

We have been working with several large corporations on their translation needs, including *contracts and agreements, HR documentation, training programs, client and employee surveys, computer-related material (websites, software localization, hardware specification, help files, user manuals, and mobile apps and games) and general business communications (newsletters and press releases, advertising and marketing).* Among our most relevant clients are The Dow Chemical Company, United Technologies Company, Daikin Industries Ltd., Thales e-Security, and Dell Computers.

Our preferred CAT Tool is Swordfish (compatible with both TMX and TXT memory files, as well as Trados TTX, Wordfast TXML, and MemoQ XLF bilingual files). Our average output is at about 350 words / hour and our current rate for this language pair is [CHECK RATES TABLE] per source word, which includes proofreading. *Discounts are available based on a CAT Tool analysis on matches ($X.XX) and repetitions ($X.XX).*

To learn more about our professional background, please refer to our business portfolio at http://www.wordawareness.com. References are available upon request.

We look forward to hearing from you,

Rafa Lombardino, C.T.

English into Portuguese / Portuguese into English
Certified by the American Translators Association (ATA)

Spanish/English Professional Certificate in
Translation by the UC San Diego Extension

Email: translations@wordawareness.com
Site: http://www.wordawareness.com
Skype: wordawareness

T: (858) 200-5844
F: (866) 896-6120

P.O. Box 710099
Santee, CA 92072-0099

The 2nd paragraph should highlight your **qualifications**. Why should they choose you? Are you a certified translator in that language pair? Do you have a professional background in that area? Have you completed several assignments that are similar to the one they have at hand?

Note that the 2nd paragraph will most likely be different in each cover letter, depending on the translation field and the language combination you are targeting. In other words, edit the template to tailor your cover letter to the specific situation.

On the 3rd paragraph, you can **mention examples** of similar projects you've completed for other clients, while keeping in mind the NDAs you've signed and how you cannot disclose information about other companies to potential competitors.

On the 4th paragraph, **close the deal**. Talk about your output, as in how many words you can translate per hour or day. Ensure that you can meet their deadline or even deliver the project earlier than expected, if that is the case. And finally inform them of your rate and/or total price for the project.

If you work with a CAT tool and decided to give discounts on matches and repetitions, let your client know about it in this paragraph as well. And while you're on the subject, tell your client the payment options you accept.

This 4th paragraph may also change according to the assignment you're trying to get. Maybe you charge different rates for different fields or language pairs, or maybe your output varies according to target language or area of specialization.

Finally, end the letter by pointing your client to your professional profile or website, and say that you can provide references upon request, if that's the case. Don't forget to end the letter with a professional signature stating your name, language pair, certificates, contact information and location, for time zone purposes.

Yet another thing you must consider when creating your cover letters is that you will save time selecting the appropriate template if you **save each file with an easy-to-spot name**. For example, "FR-ES HR" would be used for French-to-Spanish

Human Resources projects, or "EN-ES Medical" for English-to-Spanish assignments related to medicine and health.

Another good idea is to make sure you **have copies accessible to you anytime and anywhere**. Consider using Google Drive or a similar cloud platform, because all you would need to do then is log into your account and your templates will be right there waiting for you. This way, you can apply for a project quickly and without forgetting any crucial information to show your competitive edge.

Lastly, here's one very important suggestion: Whether you're working as a freelancer or representing your own translation business, make sure you use the correct tone when applying for a project. **Avoid words like "position," "opening," and "employment,"** because this would give potential clients the idea that you wish to become an employee at their company, when they're actually looking for a contractor who will be assisting them on an as-needed basis. These are so-called "turn-off words" because it would imply that you wish to earn salary plus benefits, as opposed to providing services in exchange for a professional fee.

✓ **QUICK TIP: If you're sending your cover letter in response to a message about a potential project and the potential client did not specify a delivery date, consider the total word count provided and use your average output to calculate how long it would take you to complete it. Then, make sure you specify exactly when you can send it back in terms of BUSINESS DAYS. This is a better approach, as opposed to mentioning a given date, because it may still take a few days until the project is approved and you receive the source material.**

CREATE YOUR BRAND AND BUSINESS IMAGE

I'm sure you've heard that an image is worth 1,000 words, right? Think about successful businesses with a loyal client base and the **image** that they use to represent themselves. It could literally be a **visual cue**, such as a logo, or a **slogan** that summarizes the company's mission statement.

Now we'll discuss how to create your **brand** and promote your services with a strong business image. Your goal will be to create something that speaks to you and can be used in all your marketing materials and online campaigns.

o   **Find a Logo That Represents Your Motto**

Let's start with an image that your client will always associate with you—not in the metaphorical sense, but as an actual logo. When trying to find the **perfect logo**, go back to your **business plan** (remember *Section 2*?) and try to associate your overall features—including your mission, specialization and target audience—with a **strong image**.

It could be something as simple and elegant as your **initials**, in case you're working as a freelancer under your own name, or your **company name** in nice lettering... That's enough to create a visual association with your name. It'll also be your identity in a world where you rarely get to meet people face to face.

If you're not very artistic, ask around for recommendations on local businesses or **freelance designers** who can listen to your ideas and create a fresh **visual concept**. Alternatively, look for online solutions that have a vast **image library**, so you can select a pre-designed item and customize it to your liking.

The good thing about logos is that you get to use them in every piece of marketing material you create to leave your mark and have a **consistent visual representation** of your professional on-line persona, which we'll talk more about in the next topic. For now, let's brainstorm the creative ways you can use your logo and reach out to potential clients during your marketing efforts.

> ✓ **QUICK TIP: Avoid using pictures you find online, because most of them are copyright protected. Check the EXTRAS in this book for sites you can visit to find good logo material for sale or images that are labeled as copyright free.**

o **Design Your Marketing Materials**

Once you have the perfect logo, pay attention to the colors you're using and establish your **color scheme**. Several articles and studies have been written on the psychological impact that colors can have—some are more soothing and reassuring, others present a call for action—so align your logo, personality, and business idea with a set of given colors or shades of the same color to create a pleasant look.

The first material you could create is a **business card** with your logo, first and last name, slogan, phone and fax numbers, email address, and location (for time zone purposes). Most importantly, add your language combination and professional certificate information (if applicable) so your potential clients may actually know what you do when they pick up your business card.

Order the minimum amount from a printing service and keep your cards with you at all times, because you never know when you'll stumble upon a business opportunity. You may meet someone at the gym, at the park, at the beach, or at a coffee shop while you're enjoying some downtime and strike up a conversation that may result in a potential lead. You can run into target customers at conferences and professional sessions, whether or not they are translation-related. Or you may find yourself in a store or restaurant that has strong links to a community that speaks your source or target language, and whose customers may require occasional translation services involving their personal documents.

Another marketing piece you can create is a **letterhead**. Place the same relevant information you used in your business card in the header or footer of a document, which you may use as a template when writing professional letters, proofreading reports, fax cover letters, and certificates of translation.

You can also create a **flyer** or **brochure** to educate your potential clients on translation or interpretation services. It's worth mentioning that you should adopt the mindset of a business person and make the most of the limited space to make a strong case for how you and/or your company can help their business. Maybe they work with suppliers in other countries, or they have international branches and need to translate their training material so workers in those locations will follow corporate procedures...

Have your target audience in mind and explain why your services will help them achieve their goals.

Odds are these clients won't be interested in CAT tools or translation theories and processes. However, if you highlight how important it is to hire a qualified language professional—just like you—to grow their business by interacting with a new undiscovered customer base or reaching out to commercial partners in other countries, they will probably get back to you.

Your marketing materials must **be concise and to the point**. After all, it is about advertising your services, so you should be colorful, go for the WOW effect, and really grab the attention of your audience. Think about your favorite commercials and try to emulate the components that make them so special to you. You could have the same effect on your clients by presenting yourself that way and making them realize they have a need for what you are offering.

Another marketing material that has been used very often nowadays is **postcards**. You can have a nice glossy image on one side, with your logo, slogan, and catchy information. And, on the back, you can have some brief information about your services and maybe offer a deal, like 10% off the first translation project. That may sound odd, like you should be working in a retail store, but it may be enough to convince a client to use your services and keep coming back for more.

Other marketing materials you may create, depending on your particular setup, include:

- **Presentation Folders** — If you're planning on scheduling meetings with companies you'd like to work with, this is a very professional way to deliver several marketing materials in one single location. It's also ideal if you're invited to be a keynote speaker and want to provide attendants with literature and notepads for them to take notes on the subject you'll be addressing.

- **Address Labels or Personalized Envelopes** — Perfect for the occasional envelope you may have to send out to clients, whether you're delivering printed copies of the translation you completed for them, a notarized certificate of translation, or a copy of your invoice, in case they don't accept electronic versions by email.

- **Sticky Notes** — You can have a stack of personalized Post-It® notes handy, in case you need to write something down (a quote, perhaps?!) and hand it to a potential business lead you're talking to in a very informal setting.

- **Holiday and Thank You Cards** — It's a great way to stay present in your client's mind during special occasions or after successfully completing a large project together.

- **Signs, Posters, and Banners** — Maybe you'll attend a conference and have an exhibitor's book, or you have an office where you can display your logo and contact info on the window or at the door. These are good attention grabbers for a place with heavy foot traffic.

- **Window Decals, Bumper Stickers, and Car Door Magnets** — If your mantra is, "We never know where we'll find our next client!" why not use your car as an advertising vehicle?

- **Tote Bags, Hats, Shirts, and Hoodies** — On that note, why not maximize your business exposure by taking your business everywhere you go? If you enjoy running or biking, wear a shirt with your company logo when you hit the gym, take the streets, or join your next race!

- **Pens, Key chains, Mugs, Phone Cases, Calendars, Can Coolers, Bottle Openers, USB Flash Drives, Stress Balls, etc.** — These are great items for you to use and display yourself, and maybe strike up a conversation about what you do for a living, or give as a gift to clients you've been working with for some time.

✓ **Check the EXTRAS in this book for sites you can use to design your marketing materials.**

So far, we've talked about printed marketing solutions, but once you have your logo, you can also **take the internet** and create an omnipresence that will be essential to reaching out to an international client base. As I mentioned a couple of times in this book already, the world is your oyster, so take advantage of technology not only to make your life easier, but to **let potential clients know you exist.**

We'll now discuss a few ideas on how to **develop your presence online, interact with others** and **position yourself as a problem-solver.**

o   **Work on your On-line Persona**

The best possible way you can market yourself is creating an on-line identity. You can start with a **professional website—** you don't need anything fancy, just a clean look with key information about your activities, how people can contact you, and the marketing materials you have created.

There are several services you can use to create your own website by yourself. Most likely, you won't be getting a professional look without some investment, though, by either dedicating time to learn how to use web platforms effectively, or hiring someone to help you achieve your goals.

There are free options you can turn to, but even the most affordable platforms will really make you stand out and have a more professional look, starting with a **domain name** that is unique to you, so you can have your own .com or .net address for both your website and email address. (Besides, who would really be interested in hiring a professional translator whose email address is hotchick1980@hotmail.com?)

Unlike printed materials, your on-line identity can reach clients anywhere in the world, instantly, and you don't have to pay extra for stamps. And now, in the era of **social networking,** it may pay off to set up professional profiles on websites like

Facebook, LinkedIn, Twitter, and even create your own channel on **YouTube**. The thing is that you never know where your next client may be, and having as many connections as possible is better than having no connections at all.

Just make sure you **act very professionally**, because you are representing your business, so try not to post pictures or comments that would compromise your on-line identity. Watch what other people in the industry are doing and learn from both the good and the bad examples.

Above all, think about something that sets you apart from the crowd. Specialization could make you stand out. Try to introduce yourself as both an expert and a language professional who will address the needs that clients may have in a particular niche. Draw from your past experiences as a student, your previous career, and your hobbies and interests to use your knowledge for your marketing advantage.

o   **Create a Website or Blog**

Your first step before you create a website for your business is to do your homework. Research other websites related to the T&I industry and write down a list of things you like and dislike about them. This exercise should give you some ideas on how to build your own **virtual office**.

Yes, I truly believe you should consider your website your "virtual office." After all, that is where clients will most likely go to "meet" you, so keep that in mind when you're organizing your space to make it pleasant-looking to visitors and help them find the information they need about your services.

If you've already worked on your business plan and brainstormed whether you'll be working under your own name or would rather register a company name, your next step is to buy that **domain name** and secure your online identity. Make it easy to remember and spell, keep it short, and avoid dashes— people may forget to type the dash and end up going to a completely different website!

Then you can roll up your sleeves and get to work. Start with a **Home Page** that could act as an attractive "book cover" to invite visitors to browse through the rest of the pages. Use your logo somewhere at the top, and follow the same color scheme you have already selected for your marketing materials to make sure everything matches and has a consistent look.

Create a **Portfolio** page, where you'd be able to display **samples** of your work and a **list of clients** you have worked with, either directly or through a translation agency—as long as you have permission to disclose their names as examples of the material you have dealt with throughout your career.

Having a separate **Services** page will allow you to explain what you do in more detail. Do you work as a translator only, or do you offer interpreting services as well? Will you be working as a proofreader or text editor, too? Do you do any technical writing or act as a language consultant? Do you have experience as a voice talent and are willing to do voice over recordings? We'll talk more about these additional services later in this section, under *Diversify Yourself.*

In order to provide even more detail about your background, you can create a **Translation Fields** page to mention your areas of expertise and give clients a better idea about the subjects you're used to working with.

✓ **QUICK TIP: Actually, this is a great way to list the type of material you've translated in each field, and then resort to it whenever you're customizing a cover letter, so you don't have to type the same examples every time you contact a potential client in that area.**

Having a **Frequently Asked Questions (FAQ)** page is also a good idea to address questions clients usually ask about how translation works. You can mention your output, your rates, the file formats you accept, whether you use any CAT tools, etc.

Think about how you would explain what you do to someone who is not used to requesting translations services, and provide details on how you work. Then, if a potential client has a question, you can always refer them to your FAQ page.

Last, but not the least, you MUST have a **Contact** page, in which you'll provide your phone and fax numbers, email, address, username for instant message services, physical address (or mailing address, if you don't have an office clients can visit,) and links to your professional profile pages on job boards or social media websites. Actually, most website platforms will also offer a contact form for visitors to send you a message, so you don't have to disclose your email address, thus minimizing spam.

And, if you're only promoting your own services, and really making yours the personal site of a professional service provider, you could even combine this Contact page with an **About Me** page, featuring a short biography and professional photo, maybe talking about how you got started, the certificates and degrees you have, among other accomplishments you'd like to share. On the other hand, if you're working with a partner or a small team, you could have an **About Us** page with a short bio and photo for each one of your team members.

Some extra pages you can create to expand on your professional website include the following:

- **Payment** — If you'll be receiving electronic payments, it's a good idea to have a page you can direct clients to. There, they'd find links, maybe even detailed instructions, on how to make payment directly to you.

- **Volunteering** — If you have donated your time as a translator and/or interpreter to a cause you'd like to talk about.

- **Links** — Share resources, like glossaries, publications, and manuals, or interesting sites and blogs.

- **Industry Jargon** — This list can complement your FAQ page, but focus specifically on the keywords we use in the T&I industry, so potential clients can understand what you're talking about.

- **Software** — This would be the list of tools you use in your daily work, including translation-specific software and other programs that you may resort to for organization and business purposes.

> ✓ **Check the EXTRAS in this book for sites you can use to design your website or blog.**

Now, when it comes to **blogging**, you can either have a blog as a section of your business website, or a separate blog with its own website address—it all depends on your own setup. The only thing you need to keep in mind is that blogging demands **dedication, time, creativity, and being up to date** on what's going on in the professional world.

According to Corinne McKay[10]—a very successful translation blogger who's been updating *Thoughts on Translation* quite regularly since 2008—if you want to start a blog, you should create an "inventory" of at least 20 articles before you even launch your site, and then keep the production going, so you never run out of posts and can keep it flowing.

If you're just getting your feet wet and still unsure whether blogging is for you, a good idea is to **write articles**, and then submit them to publications like the *ATA Chronicle* or *Translation Journal*, or to bloggers who may feature you as a **guest blogger** on their own website. This way, you don't have to

---

[10] MCKAY, Corinne. *Want to Start a Blog? Write 20 Posts!*, Thoughts on Translation, March 19, 2010: http://bit.ly/T3-20BlogPosts

keep your production up, and only write sporadically when you feel the urge to address a subject in particular.

Here are some general topics that you can explore and write about to offer your perspective as a professional translator or interpreter on the state of our industry:

- Educating clients on what T&I is all about

- Case studies detailing what a successful translator-client collaboration entails

- Interviews with professionals working in the field

- Examples of how unsupervised machine translations aren't the most suitable option for a reputable business to reach out to foreign clients or partners

- Examples of good and bad translations, with images to draw more interest of the audience

- Commentary on news coverage involving issues that affect translators and interpreters

---

✓ **Check the EXTRAS in this book for translation publication websites you may already enjoy reading, but maybe can now contribute to with your own articles as well.**

---

o **Join Social Networking Websites**

As mentioned several times on these pages, social networking is a very important tool to expand your on-line reach. Many people are still uncomfortable using **Facebook**, **Twitter**, even **LinkedIn**, but these and many other social media websites will only help you if you know how to use them correctly for your business purposes.

These websites can be used to **spread news** about your company, your volunteering efforts, articles you've written for your own blog or as a guest blogger on someone else's website, and to share general information about the industry to motivate a debate among your peers.

You can also use social networking to keep tabs on potential clients. For example, Twitter has a resource called **Lists** that doesn't seem to be used as often as it should. Basically, you can add a Twitter profile to a list, let's say, of "Translation Agencies," or "Medical Companies," or "Book Publishers," whatever your interest may be. This way, you'll compile a roster of individual and businesses to keep an eye on, because they're potential clients or may provide leads on your field of expertise.

> ✓ **REMEMBER: The time of the Rolodex® and address books is over! Find creative ways to keep in touch with potential clients by engaging them online.**

On the other end of the spectrum, social networks can also help you **scout for partners**, that is, like-minded professionals who may be of help when you are assigned a large project or would like an extra set of eyes to look over your work.

Even though translating sounds like a pretty isolated activity when you're working from home all by yourself, that doesn't mean you're all alone. More than ever, freelancers can now make work a lot easier on themselves by finding allies to help them solve their dilemmas—of a language or business nature—or share experiences about what they've learned throughout their careers. The internet will put you **in touch with people like you, who are passionate** about languages and trying to turn their skills into a profitable business.

Join **web communities**, **discussion forums**, and **professional groups** to find people who could be potential collaborators. A good way to interact and learn more about one another is to **set up a large volunteering assignment**, maybe by making a news article available in a platform like Google Drive, and tackling it as a group to address a cause you all hold dear to your hearts.

And, since you don't have to be limited to your connectivity, join your **local translation association** and sign up for **seminars** and **conferences** to get out of the office, meet some people—maybe put a face to a name you already know from the virtual world—then network and exchange experiences in the real world as well.

Lastly, remember you must always keep a neutral tone, because you're representing your business, and should build a good, positive image. Many people seem to forget that **the same etiquette you use during face-to-face interactions also apply to on-line conversations**.

> ✓ **Check SECTION 4 to learn what newcomers think about social networking.**

o   Diversify Yourself

Let's face it: **Working as a freelancer is always a risky business**. Until you're able to get a steady workflow to keep you busy and secure an income, you may have to hold a part-time job, rely on your partner (or parents) with a "regular job," or tackle different tasks to fill in the gaps in your schedule. Still, this is a somewhat unstable market and you're bound to experience ups and downs throughout your career. In other words, you must find ways to diversify yourself and your income to keep your business sustainable.

As discussed earlier (*Negotiation Skills — How to Calculate Your Rates: Types of Services,*) you can offer additional language-related services on top of only translating or interpreting. You can also be a:

- **Proofreader or Copyeditor** — Read other people's work, whether it is translated or original material, to correct spelling and grammar, and give overall feedback on how to improve their writing.

- **Reviewer or Validator** — Consider addressing the large demand of some translation agencies that need an extra set of eyes not only during "live projects," but also to scout the market for freelancers and analyze samples to confirm whether a translator would be a good addition to the team.

- **Consultant** — Join forces with companies that plan to invest in or expand to a foreign market. As a professional bilingual, you would be in a great position to offer insight about the language and cultural aspects of the location your client is targeting, given your experiences with the respective country and its people, thus helping a company decide whether their approach, products or services are effective and match the foreign market's expectations.

- **Voice Artist** — Record audio for companies interested in catering to their foreign audience, including messages for their customer service hotline and voice over for videos.

- **Teacher** — Once you've spent a few years enjoying a successful career, share what you've learned to pass your knowledge along. Maybe you could give practical tips on how to run a translation business, focus on specific vocabulary used in your area, or explore translation techniques to help your peers working in the same language combination.

- **Speaker** — Similarly to being an Instructor, you can share your experiences in short-term efforts, like webinars and conferences, and special events.

These additional tasks—which are still related to your main activity—will only contribute to your career, "beef up" your resume, and diversify your income, in addition to building a strong reputation for yourself and your business.

○ **The Downside of Living Online**

The last topic I'd like to address in *Leave Your Mark Online* is the issue that everybody seems to fear: **The negative effects of being exposed to the entire world on the internet.**

We've talked about how you can control your own actions and disclose only as much information as you feel comfortable doing. However, when you "put yourself out there," you may end up getting unwanted results from that exposure. The best way for you to protect yourself is to anticipate the worst, so you can prepare for it, while hoping for the best—always.

For example, you may encounter clients who will try to scam a group of translators in order to **get a job done for free**. This may come as short "samples" sent out to several candidates and that, in reality, are different paragraphs of the same document. Since many clients request free samples in order to evaluate your work and check whether you're the best match for their project, you may participate in such a scam unknowingly.

One way to avoid it is to keep an eye on discussion forums and have a close-knit group of like-minded professionals who work into your target language and may end up being recruited to work on the same material, while translating different "samples" of the complete document. If you notice that people are talking about a project of a similar nature to yours, or even asking for help with terminology that you've been looking up yourself while working on your sample, be on high alert and **initiate an open discussion about your suspicions**. "Are you also translating material about XYZ?"

In this first scenario, besides the feeling of being scammed and the time that you may have dedicated to contacting the potential client to introduce yourself and then considering the sample translation you were going to work on, at least you wouldn't have gone through irreparable harm. However, **when clients never had any intention of paying you in the first place** after you've completed a project, that's where the harm is.

You're doing the right thing if you're making yourself accessible, so clients can learn about your services if they look you up online. However, this is a two-way road, and you should also take the time to know your potential clients better.

As we already covered earlier (*Negotiation Skills — Invoicing Practices,*) if they are an individual, ask for payment in advance—tell them it's your company policy, if you must. However, in this second scenario, if it is a company hiring your services, make sure you do a **background check** on them as well by going to their website, looking up where their offices are located, and maybe even giving them a quick call to thank them for reaching out and entrusting you with their project.

You should also look the company name up on job boards and other websites that feature a **"blacklist" of bad payers**. This way, you'll be able to read the feedback of other translators who have worked with them. And, remember that close-knit group of like-minded professionals I've just mentioned? Well, you can always ask the colleagues you trust whether they've had any experiences with your potential client.

These are simple steps you can take to protect yourself against scammers who sound legitimate, but don't want to pay for your hard work. Now, I know this may sound highly paradoxical, considering what I just said about working with individuals, but another red flag you should consider is when a client—most likely an individual—offers to pay for your services in advance.

In this third scenario, which is a modified **Nigerian scam** targeting freelancers, so-called clients contact you with a document, most likely about a topic they'll be presenting at a conference or similar event. Your interaction with them will usually include these tell-tales:

- First of all, their English is very poor and the message is full of typos and grammar mistakes—which aren't necessarily a red flag if you're interacting with a non-English speaker, but once you read quite a few of those messages, you quickly find a pattern in language and message formatting.

- They say they'll do a presentation in a country that doesn't quite match the language combination they're requesting—that is, if they do mention a language combination at all...

- The deadline is very generous, usually months away for a relatively small file you could complete in a week or so.

- You look up a couple of sentences from the material and find a few webpages that display the entire document online—odds are they copied something very general about environment, child development, or business management from an existing website.

- They mention they'll be out of the country for the next few weeks, but a secretary/partner will follow up on it with you.

- They offer to pay in advance and request your address to mail you a check.

- When the check arrives, you notice that the total amount is almost two or three times what you originally quoted.

- A secretary/partner does follow up with you, saying that a clerical error was made and that, if you don't mind, you can go ahead and cash the check anyway (The main person who signed the check is out of the country, remember? So they unfortunately can't issue a new one right away...) then you can return the difference to them through Western Union.

Freelancers who are eager to secure their next project, or are yet inexperienced in the industry, usually jump at this opportunity and trustingly return the difference to their client. Then, they come to realize that **the check was fake all along**, that their bank was never able to clear it, and they'll never again see the money they wired to their so-called client.

One way to confirm this to be a scam is paying close attention to the check you've been sent. If you're not familiar with the bank name, research it online, because some scammers use old checks from banks that no longer exist. If it is from a bank you recognize, pay attention to check properties, such as the image of a little lock that is sensitive to temperature and should disappear if you blow some hot air directly into it. Sometimes the check may visually seem legitimate, so you can always go to the nearest branch of that bank and see if they can verify it for you.

Moving on to the fourth and last scenario I'd like to mention as one of the downsides of "living online," this one has potential for a more long-lasting harm. It's the so-feared case of **identity theft**, and it may come in two different shapes: on the one hand, it may be as a result of a scammer finding your resume online; on the other hand, a scammer may pretend to be a legitimate client and ask for a copy of your resume, along with the **unusual request that you sign an agreement allowing their company to submit your resume** to thousands of their clients who have amazing opportunities waiting for you...

If you're ever contacted by someone mentioning this kind of agreement, run to the hills! This is a relatively new technique that scammers are using to get a hold of your resume—if it's not easily found online—so that they can make a copy of it, **change your contact information and pass for you** when negotiating with clients. In other words, they use your good credentials and experiences to get a client. You never get to hear about it, since the client will have contacted a fake email address. Then, scammers most likely completes the job in a language they do not speak by using machine translation and deliver it to the client as if it were your own work. And, of course, they will cash in using your name, and tainting your reputation in the process.

These four scenarios are certainly stuff out of nightmares for independent professionals like us. Nevertheless, **these horror stories are not enough to justify your lack of online presence**. On the contrary, if you have a strong presence online, odds are it'll be harder to use your identity convincingly. For example, if you use your own domain name in your professional email address—in other words, your very own brand name—any address using a free account and your name might end up raising suspicions.

It may sound vain, but if you **google yourself regularly**, or even set up **news alerts for every time your name is mentioned somewhere**, you'll be able to identify when your name has been used improperly. And, should you find an email address attached to your name, but which you have not created yourself, be proactive about it and display it prominently (in a footnote under your email signature, on the top of your resume, on a professional profile page, and on your website, for example) to let clients know that anyone contacting them using that email DOES NOT represent you. If you're very vocal about it, including an article you may write about your negative experience, you'll be taking back your identity and reputation.

Sometimes this kind of scam is a little harder to detect, because the scammer may not use your name or combine parts of your resume with that of another translator, creating something hybrid under a fake name. In order to find out if you've been the victim of this kind of identity theft, or even to report a similar case that happened to you or a colleague, I highly advise you to visit Translator-Scammers.com, a very important effort aimed at outing scammers and setting the record straight.

Lastly, this is something that doesn't target translators and freelancers only, but internet users in general: **Beware of phishing**! This technique is used when scammers email you a link (or maybe post it to a social media account they invaded and that belongs to an unsuspecting friend or relative of yours) and, when you click that link, you're taken to a fake website that may look just like the real thing. It could be an exact copy of your bank's login page, maybe an innocent-looking survey, or anything that would request your personal information (name, password, account number, social security number, etc.) which would later be used to invade your account and have access to your finances.

The same way you wouldn't provide information over the phone without being sure that the person on the other end of the line is legitimate, don't do it online, even if the page looks harmless or familiar to you.

HOW TO USE JOB BOARDS

After exploring some ideas on how to work on your online presence on a very macro sense—that is, leaving your professional mark on the internet—let's take a few steps back and target your efforts towards clients who already have an existing need for your services.

You can find such clients in **job boards** dedicated to translation or freelancing in general, where you can create your **professional profile** as part of your marketing efforts, and then use it when **applying for projects**.

○   **What Job Boards Have to Offer**

Before we go deeper into creating a professional profile and applying for projects, there are a few things you need to know about using job boards. Your success in being assigned a project unfortunately will not depend entirely on your qualifications and how effective your profile is.

Perhaps the most relevant aspect of competing for a job online is actually your language pair and, consequently, how many people have registered at the website with a similar profile. **The more unique a language combination is**—let's say Chinese into Catalan or Flemish into Japanese—**the less competition someone will have.**

But there's no need to worry if yours is a popular language pair, though. Odds are **if there is an abundance of supply, there could also be a high demand**. And, in these cases, specialization is key, as we've talked about earlier in this section. If you keep your marketing materials sharp, create a thorough profile, and have confidence in your expertise, your chances will be pretty good.

Overall, job boards are very similar. They allow companies and individuals who already have a need for language services to post a job opportunity online. They also allow talents to create a professional profile and showcase their services.

Some of these sites are fancier than others, as they will function as a **one-stop shop that offers several solutions**, allowing you to set up your own personal website and email inbox, keep a virtual wallet to receive electronic payments, and publish your availability schedule and rates sheet.

Most job boards have **discussion forums**, so you can interact with other translators and talk about the trials and errors of our profession, or get hands-on tips on several issues we face every day. A few sites have **opinion polls and articles** written by site members, so you can have a better understanding of what your peers expect from the T&I industry and have achieved in their careers.

Some of these websites will also have a **community glossary** section, where you can look up words or expressions and even submit questions and get help from other translators.

✓ **QUICK TIP: When researching terminology on community glossaries, it is recommended to always take suggestions with a grain of salt. You should see this source of information as your starting point and do your own research before reaching a final conclusion. In other words, don't trust anyone blindly, especially if the website where you found a glossary or term gives members participation points for their activity.**

A few job boards partner with **companies that offer products or services** to language professionals, so that you can enter into a group-buy deal and purchase a **CAT tool license at a discounted price**, for example, or participate in **training sessions** that are affordable or completely free of charge.

As translation and interpretation continues to become a popular career, websites like these will pop up left and right, because people seem to be increasingly more aware of how profitable this industry can be. So, my personal suggestion is that you search for new venues periodically to create an account and have a personalized page up on as many websites as possible. It's also good to review your profile from time to time in order to add fresh data and keep everything up to date.

After becoming more familiar with these sites, you can decide where to invest your time and money. The downside is that some of these websites will request that you pay a **monthly or yearly premium** in order to actually contact clients directly. Some are pricier than others, so you'll need to balance your needs with your budget and analyze what the site has to offer. With that in mind, one good feature is that a few job boards will have special deals and give you points for your participation on the site, so you may end up getting a discount on your premium.

> ✓ **Check the EXTRAS in this book for job boards you can visit to create your professional profile.**

On another note, keep in mind that **one of the main controversial points regarding job boards is the rate** individuals charge for their services. There are endless forum threads on the subject, some clients will post job announcements and tell you upfront how much they're willing to pay, and many translators and interpreters will publish their desired rates in their profiles and websites.

Odds are you will be caught in the middle of a crossfire. You will feel uncomfortable and confused.

- "Isn't this client offering too little for so much work?"

- "How can I compete with this translator who has a profile similar to mine, but charges ¼ of my rate?"

- "Am I the one charging too little, 'cause that other translator's rate is three times higher than mine!"

This will most likely be an endless debate. **There will always be translators charging less than you do.** Maybe they work faster and can make just as much at the end of the day. Maybe the cost of living where they are located is lower, so they can pay their bills and save money by charging two-thirds of your rate. **The very opposite is true about those who charge more than you do.** They may have higher expenses or a very hard-to-find expertise that justifies their price tag.

You'll also find that **some clients want to pay almost close to nothing** for translation services, which may happen for one of the following two reasons:

a) They are **completely uninformed** about how translations actually work and haven't considered all the effort that goes into being faithful to the original message and, at the same time, appealing to the international audience speaking the target language,

or

b) They are **willing to sacrifice quality** in order to meet their budget, thus hurting their own business, whether or not they are aware of it.

Notwithstanding their reasons to offer little compensation, it is your duty as a translator to work hard on client education and let them know the added-value you have to offer. Remember to always be professional without sounding condescending. **Being straightforward and open to negotiation will take you a long way,** so keep in mind this is supposed to be a two-way relationship in which clients need your help and you need clients in order to have a sustainable work flow.

On the other end of the spectrum, clients who make an informed decision about what language services are really about will be willing to pay you for your time and build a long-term relationship with you.

The best advice I can give you when you're first exposed to the world of on-line job boards is not to get overwhelmed. **Do your own thing**, keep contacting clients, applying for projects, networking, and improving your skills. **A perfect match will finally come along** and one project alone may pay for everything you've invested into your business and then some. Or, even better, you can get a reliable client for life—literally.

> ✓ **REMEMBER: The only proactive approach you can take when talking to clients who don't really understand the T&I industry is to educate them. The American Translators Association (ATA) has a couple of brochures about client education, which you may recommend to your potential clients, so they have a better perspective of what your services represent to their business. Check the EXTRAS in this book for links to these resources.**

Talking about rates and payment, yet another great benefit of belonging to some job boards are areas called "blueboard" or "black and white list," where translators publish **information about good and bad payers**. You can save yourself a lot of headaches by avoiding clients with a negative history.

o   **Create Professional Profiles**
Most beginners don't feel ready to have a website quite yet, and that's okay—you gotta take small steps towards your marketing goals, and building a website is definitely a big step! However, that doesn't mean you should have zero presence online. At a minimum, you can create professional profiles to highlight your experiences, and then use them as some sort of **"online business card"** that you can send to potential clients to introduce yourself and help them learn more about you and how you can help their business succeed.

Still, don't think that, once your profile is up, you'll start receiving tons of messages with interesting project offers. It doesn't quite work like that. You must promote your services by applying for projects posted on these websites, in order to **call the attention of clients who are already looking for someone** like you to complete a given task.

✓ **Check SECTION 4 to learn how newcomers wish to integrate job boards into their routine.**

First of all, you must set up a user account, which is simple enough, but still requires a little bit of forethought. As I mentioned before, just as you must create a professional email address for business purposes, **your username also needs to be something trustworthy**, because that's what clients will see and identify with your profile. Your first and last name is a good start, of course, but it could also be your business name, unless the job board in question allows you to create a professional profile for yourself as an individual, then a separate page inside your profile with information about your company. Having said that, avoid nicknames, numbers, symbols and marketing gimmicks. Keep it simple.

Then it's time to select an image that will represent you on the website. I can't emphasize it enough that you'll be using this kind of profile for PROFESSIONAL purposes, so do yourself a favor and **avoid unprofessional pictures**—which potential clients will remember for all the wrong reasons.

✓ **QUICK TIP: It's always a good idea to use some sort of password management application, or at least a spreadsheet, to keep a list of all your profiles, including each direct internet address (URL) and respective username and passwords.**

Here is some practical advice when it comes to your photo:

DON'T TO DO THIS	DO THIS INSTEAD
Don't use images of your pets or children. We all know you love them, but keep them in your personal albums.	This profile is about YOU, a professional who is responsible, trustworthy, and will get the job done.
Don't cut yourself out of a group picture. There's always someone else's hand, arm, leg or cheek getting in the way.	It's okay to use an informal picture of you at a nice location, let's say, during your last vacation, for example.
Don't post pictures of you wearing something "too revealing." You sure may look good, but if you wouldn't wear that outfit at an office job, odds are it doesn't belong in your professional profile either.	Go for business casual, at most. Have a "clean look" (discrete makeup and well-trimmed facial hair) and make sure the patterns on your shirt or jacket, and accessories like ties and jewelry, aren't distracting.
Don't use moving gifs under any circumstance. We're not in the 1990s anymore!	A picture of you sitting in your office or with a pleasant background is enough.
Selfies are okay, but please don't make a duck face! Save it for partying with friends or gym pictures.	Wear your most welcoming and confident smile that shows you'll be there for your clients when they need you.
In some very special cases, it pays off to use a picture that is relevant to your background. Do you specialize in Medicine, Engineering, or Chemistry? If so, there's nothing wrong with wearing a white coat, a hard hat, or safety goggles in your photo.	

Now you're ready to start filling in all the information that that a job board requires of you in order to put your profile together, including:

- **Language combinations** — The most crucial information you can provide!

- **Contact information** — Email, phone and fax numbers, username for instant message programs, mailing address, and website.

- **Location** — For time zone purposes.

- **Availability** — Your working hours, when clients are welcome to contact you and expect a prompt reply.

- **Years of Experience** — When you started working as a translator/interpreter.

- **Areas of expertise** — What subjects you cover.

- **Services offered** — Are you diversifying yourself?

- **Rates** — If you wish to disclose your per-word or per-hour minimum rate.

- **Resume** — You can choose to attach a copy of your current resume to your profile.

- **Certificates** — Are you certified by a T&I organization?

- **Educational Background** — Other degrees you may have, even the ones not related to translation directly.

- **Professional Associations** — Do you belong to any?

- **Financial Information** — Tax ID #, VAT #, PayPal ID, payment method and currencies accepted.

- **Computer Specifications** — Operating system (whether you use Windows, Mac or Linux,) internet speed, general and translation-specific software.

- **Samples** — Keep in mind all the NDAs you have signed with your current clients. If you can't disclose any material, use news articles in your areas of expertise.

- **Project History** — A list of jobs you've been assigned through the website in question.

- **Teams** — Some job boards allow you to create a team if you've worked with other users in a collective project.

- **Volunteering Efforts** — Have you dedicated some of your time as a translator/interpreter?

- **Forum Posts** — Your history of interaction with other website users in discussion boards.

- **Glossaries** — Some job boards have a glossary creation function, to which you can add terms manually or upload a spreadsheet.

- **Articles** — Some job boards allow you to post articles to their collective knowledge base.

- **Professional Events** — Conferences and seminars you've attended, and sessions you may have presented.

- **Reputation Board** — Feedback that clients/colleagues have left about you, and the feedback you've given, too.

> ✓ **REMEMBER: Other than your own website, this kind of profile is the ideal place to list every single detail about your professional life, especially what did not fit into your resume.**

Once you filled in all the information, the job board will display your profile according to the page template they use. Be sure to **bookmark your unique profile address**, so you can use it in your marketing efforts. Pay special attention to it, because you may be saving a general address that will direct clients to the job board itself, where they could end up finding someone else to work on their project—and you definitely want to avoid that, right?! To test your profile address, try using another internet browser, in which you're not logged into the job board, or email the URL to a couple of friends and ask whether they can see your information.

o **Apply for Translation Projects Online**

Once you have your professional profile ready to go, make sure you set your email preferences to receive alerts whenever a project is posted in your language pair and specialization.

Keep in mind that **job boards work 24/7**, considering the fact that they bring together clients and translators living in different locations, with different time zones. In other words, a **great project may be posted while you're out of the office** and, when you finally have a chance to click the link on the email alert, it will be long gone because other people had a chance to apply for it earlier than you.

Having said that, organization is key in order to respond to job alerts promptly. As we've seen in in the beginning of this book (*Speed is Key in the Translation Industry — Allocate Time For Clerical Duties*) it is a good idea to plan your project management duties to give yourself enough time throughout the day to reply to messages about new and potential projects.

When you identify projects you're interested in, you must contact the potential client to apply for it. Unless the job poster requested that applications be sent to a direct message or have their own system available on their website, thus providing an e-mail address or link, respectively, the job board will most likely ask you to fill in a form with the following information:

- **Subject** — A general introduction that will grab the potential client's attention. For example, you can use something like *"ATA-Certified EN>PTbr Translator, 17 yrs exp., degree in Computer Sciences"* to apply for a technology project targeted at the Brazilian market; that is, as long as your credentials, years of experience, and degree in the applicable field are true and relevant to the project, of course.

- **Body of Text** — This is a great opportunity to use your cover letter template and modify it according to the details that the job poster has provided. You'll soon notice how valuable these templates can be, once you start to apply for several projects and realize you don't have to reinvent the wheel each time.

- **Language Pairs** — In case more than one combination is being requested.

- **Rate** — You can mention your complete price for the project or your per-hour or per-word rate.

- **Delivery** — When you would return the translated file.

- **Resume** — You can select whether you want to submit the resume that the website has on file, or upload the most current version you have.

After you submit your application, it's out of your hands. It will become a waiting game if don't have anything else going on, especially if it's a project you'd really like to work on. My personal advice to you is to **keep yourself preoccupied**, apply for other projects, take care of your marketing efforts, and look into building that website you may be putting off. **Job posters will select a translator based on their own needs** and you may not be a match for them for several reasons, so learn how to hear "No" and move on. Dealing with rejection and diversifying yourself is a good strategy to keep things going in this industry.

A BEGINNER'S PROFILE

In this last section of the book, we'll be discussing the profile of beginning translators. The data shown in the next few pages is the result of my observations while teaching a ten-week online class called "Tools and Technology in Translation" as part of the Professional Certificate in English/Spanish Translation and Interpretation offered by the University of California, San Diego Extension.

After interacting with 188 students in the span of four years—thirteen quarters total, from Spring 2010 through Spring 2014, with two simultaneous classes during Summer 2011—I was able to draw conclusions from their responses to surveys that were part of their homework and find the most prominent similarities among beginning translators. **It was my turn to learn from them and get a sense of their perspectives** about the T&I industry and how they fit in.

On the following pages, we'll talk about the **skills they currently have** and believe to contribute to their future career, as well as the **skills they wish to develop** in order to become better professionals; where they stand as far as their **computer knowledge** and what sort of **technology challenges** they believe they'll be facing; how comfortable they are with **social networking**; what they intend to use **online job boards** for; if they plan to **volunteer** their time, and whether they see **CAT tools** and **machine translation** in their future.

Most of these survey questions were open-ended, which means students wrote in their own answers, instead of selecting options that had already been laid out for them. Others, such as skills to acquire, technology challenges, and job board use were questions focusing on four statements in particular, which they needed to order from 1 to 4, according to what they considered to be the most to the least relevant item to them.

CURRENT / FUTURE SKILLS

The very first question I ask students as part of their homework during our first week together is to **list five skills they currently have** and believe to be relevant to their career as translators and/or interpreters. Then I ask them to think about **five skills they wish to develop** during formal training or in practice, which they believe are important to become better at what they will set out to do.

○ Current Skills

After compiling 982 answers about their current skills—some students listed more than five items—and organizing them into 48 standardized items, it was time to divide the list into five main categories: **Language** (11 items), **Business** (15), **Personality** (15), **Technology** (4), and **Communication** (3).

Their answers show that students put more emphasis on their current language skills, listing their **language background and appreciation** (59 answers), as well as **writing** (45), **grammar** (41) and **reading** (41) skills as important.

Considering their business skills—the second category students feel more confident in—they say they already are **organized** (87), good at **networking** (47), and wish to seek **continuing education opportunities** (32). Some also emphasized **work ethics** (29) and **specialized knowledge** (21) as two valuable assets.

As far as personality traits—the third category with the most answers—they highlighted being **detail-oriented** (63), **self-motivated** (47), and **analytical** (11) as great advantages to their future career in T&I.

According to their answers, they also feel somewhat comfortable with their current technology skills, especially in regards to **researching** (77) different subjects and **general use of the computer** (45).

Likewise, they believe their ability to **communicate well** (36), **cultural sensitivity** (25), and **collaboration skills** (17) will contribute to their activities.

Here is how their answers were broken down, followed by charts representing their current skills in the five main categories and as a standard list:

Language-Related Skills	313 answers
Language Background / Appreciation	59
Writing Skills	45
Grammar Skills / Vocabulary	41
Reading Skills (Interpretation / Appreciation)	41
Spanish Skills	39
English Skills	32
First Language skills	18
Second Language Skills	14
Translation Skills	11
Editing / Proofreading Skills	10
Interpretation Skills	3

Business Skills	292 answers
Organization Skills	87
Networking / Public Relations / People Skills	47
Continued Ed / Eagerness to Learn	32
Work Ethics / Professional / Responsible / Reliable	29
Specialized Knowledge & Background	21
Punctuality / Meeting Deadlines	15
Problem-Solving / Resourcefulness / Working Under Pressure	14
Business Skills	10
Project Management Skills	10
Customer Service / Good Listener	9
Time Management Skills	6
Negotiation Skills	4
Generalization (vs. Specialization)	3
Marketing Skills	3
Fast Worker	2

Personality Traits	170 answers
Detail-Oriented	63
Self-Motivated / Driven / Disciplined / Dedicated	47
Analytical Skills / Good Judgment	11
Adaptability & Flexibility / Open Minded	10
Artistic / Creative / Energetic	7
Patient	5
Accurate / Perfectionist / Precise	4
Methodical / Following Directions / Strategic	5
Multitasker	4
Ambitious / Goal-Oriented / Risk Taker	3
Leadership Skills	3
Life Experience / Well-Rounded	3
Confident	2
Optimist	2
Memory (Recall / Retention)	1

Technology Skills	129 answers
Research Skills	77
Computer Skills / Technologically Savvy	45
Typing Skills	4
Translation Tools (CAT)	3

Communications	78 answers
Communication Skills	36
Cultural Sensitivity	25
Collaboration Skills	17

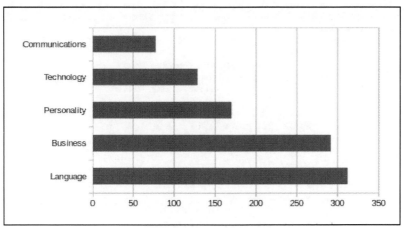

**CURRENT SKILLS CHART
BY CATEGORY**

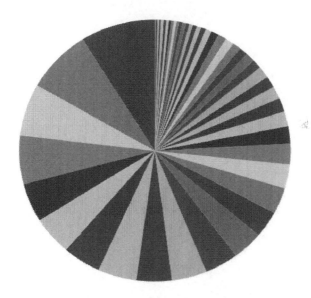

**CURRENT SKILLS CHART
BY SKILLS**

For full-color charts, visit http://www.RafaLombardino.com/tools

- Organization Skills
- Research Skills
- Detail-Oriented
- Language Background / Appreciation
- Networking / Public Relations / People Skills
- Self-motivation / Drive / Discipline / Dedication
- Computer Skills / Technologically Savvy
- Writing Skills
- Grammar Skills / Vocabulary
- Reading Skills (Interpretation / Appreciation)
- Spanish Skills
- Communication skills
- Continued Ed / Eagerness to Learn
- English Skills
- Work Ethics / Professional / Responsible / Reliable
- Cultural Awareness
- Specialized Knowledge & Background
- First Language skills
- Collaboration Skills / Team Player
- Punctuality / Meeting Deadlines
- Problem-Solving / Resourcefulness / Working Under Pressure
- Second Language Skills
- Analytical Skills / Good Judgment
- Translation Skills
- Adaptability & Flexibility / Open Minded
- Business skills
- Editing / Proofreading Skills
- Project Management
- Customer Service / Good Listener
- Artistic / Creative / Energetic
- Time Management Skills
- Methodical / Following Directions / Strategic
- Patient
- Accurate / Perfectionist / Precise
- Multitasking
- Negotiation Skills
- Typing Skills
- Ambitious / Goal-Oriented / Risk Taker
- Generalization (vs. Specialization)
- Interpretation Skills
- Leadership
- Life Experience / Well-Rounded
- Marketing Skills
- Translation Tools (CAT)
- Confidence
- Fast Worker
- Optimism
- Memory (Recall / Retention)

For full-color charts, visit http://www.RafaLombardino.com/tools

○ Future Skills

After compiling 982 answers about the skills they wish to acquire or develop—some students listed more than five items—and organizing them into 51 standardized items, it was time to divide the list into the same five main categories: **Business** (20 items), **Technology** (7), **Language** (13), **Personality** (8), and **Communication** (3).

Their answers show that students are eager to acquire business skills in order to trace a path for their career. They mentioned **general business skills** (71 answers), **organization skills** (55), and **networking** (46) as the areas they wish to develop the most—even though they had listed "being organized" and "good at networking" as two of the assets they were already bringing to the table.

Considering the technology-related knowledge they want to have in order to be better prepared to act as translators—the second category students pointed out as important—the overwhelming item they highlighted was learning more about **Translation Tools (CATs)**, which actually got the most mentions out of the entire survey (103). They are also concerned with general **computer skills** (76) and **research skills** (56)—even though they had originally highlighted these two items as their strengths as well.

As far as language-specific skills, they wish to **acquire vocabulary and specific terminology** (41) and develop their overall **translation skills** (32). Interestingly enough, in a certificate that focuses on English and Spanish and whose majority of students have Spanish as their A / Target language, a lot more students pointed out that they wanted to strengthen their **Spanish skills** (31) rather than their **English skills** (9).

On the personality category, they wish to **become more confident, have more drive, and a go-get attitude** (14) **be more accurate and precise while remaining neutral** (9), and **pay more attention to detail** (7).

Finally, they believe they must **become better team players** (15), improve their **communication skills** (13) and be **more culturally aware** (5) in order to improve themselves as translators and interpreters.

Here is how their answers were broken down, followed by charts representing their future skills in the five main categories and as a standard list:

Business Skills	421 answers
Business Skills	71
Organization Skills	55
Networking / Public Relations / People Skills / Social Media	46
Marketing Skills (Portfolio / Resume)	42
Output (Identify / Improve)	40
Specialization (Find / Develop)	36
Negotiation Skills / Setting Rates	33
Time Management Skills	25
Project Management	23
Finding Clients / Jobs	12
Problem-Solving / Resourcefulness / Working Under Pressure	9
Certification	7
Continued Ed / Eagerness to Learn	6
Work Ethics / Professional Demeanor	5
Punctuality / Meeting Deadlines	3
Decision-Making Skills	2
Generalization (vs. Specialization)	2
Knowledge of the Industry	2
Government Contracts	1
Teaching	1

Technology	254 answers
Translation Tools (CAT)	103
Computer Skills	76
Research Skills / Tools	56
On-line Skills / Blogging	9
Translation Tools (MT and CAT)	6
Localization Skills	2
Typing Skills	2

Language	230 answers
Vocabulary Acquisition / Terminology	41
Translation Skills	32
Spanish Skills	31
Grammar Skills	26
Language Skills / Acquisition	26
Writing Skills	25
Editing / Proofreading Skills	11
English Skills	9
Reading Skills (Patience / Interest)	9
Interpretation Skills	8
Target Language Skills	6
Source Language Skills	3
Verbal Skills / Speaking Effectively	3

Personality	44 answers
Confidence / Drive / Go-Get Attitude	14
Accurate / Precise / Remaining Neutral	9
Detail-Oriented	7
Patient	4
Methodical / Following Directions	3
Multitasker	3
Artistic / Creative	2
Memory (Recall / Retention)	2

Communications	33 answers
Collaboration Environment / Team Player	15
Communication Skills	13
Cultural Awareness	5

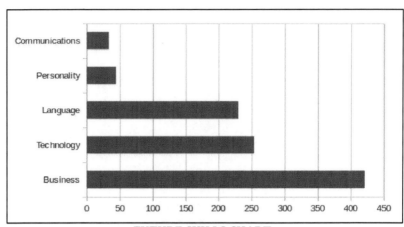

FUTURE SKILLS CHART
BY CATEGORY

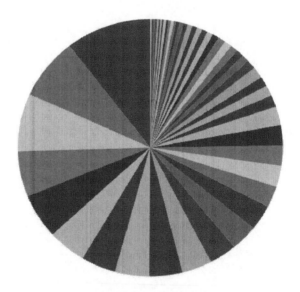

FUTURE SKILLS CHART
BY SKILLS

For full-color charts, visit http://www.RafaLombardino.com/tools

---

- Translation Tools (CAT)
- Computer Skills
- Business Skills
- Research Skills / Tools
- Organization Skills
- Networking / Public Relations / People Skills / Social Media
- Marketing Skills (Portfolio / Resume)
- Vocabulary Acquisition / Terminology
- Output (Identify / Improve)
- Specialization (Find / Develop)
- Negotiation Skills / Setting Rates
- Translation Skills
- Spanish Skills
- Grammar Skills
- Language Skills / Acquisition
- Time Management Skills
- Writing Skills
- Project Management
- Collaboration Environment / Team Player
- Communication Skills
- Finding Clients / Jobs
- Confidence / Drive / Go-Get Attitude
- Editing / Proofreading Skills
- Accurate / Precise / Remaining Neutral
- English Skills
- On-line Skills / Blogging
- Problem Solving / Resourcefulness / Working Under Pressure
- Reading Skills (Patience / Interest)
- Interpretation Skills
- Certification
- Detail-Oriented
- Continued Ed / Eagerness to Learn
- Target Language Skills
- Translation Tools (MT and CAT)
- Cultural Awareness
- Work Ethics / Professional Demeanor
- Patient
- Methodical / Following Directions
- Multitasker
- Punctuality / Meeting Deadlines
- Source Language Skills
- Verbal Skills / Speaking Effectively
- Artistic / Creative
- Decision-Making Skills
- Generalization (vs. Specialization)
- Knowledge of the Industry
- Localization Skills
- Memory (Recall / Retention)
- Typing Skills
- Government Contracts
- Teaching

For full-color charts, visit http://www.RafaLombardino.com/tools

These findings are consistent with another survey question that had them list four statements from 1 through 4, according to what they considered the most relevant (#1) and the least relevant (#4) skills they need to develop as translators.

As it happened with the open-ended question about current and future skills, 103 students mentioned CAT Tools as the most important specialized knowledge they wished to develop.

SKILLS TO ACQUIRE	# 1	# 2	# 3	# 4	Totals
CAT Tools	103	31	26	31	191
Organization and Business	49	43	61	36	189
Researching	32	52	40	65	189
Project Management	22	64	57	47	190

Note: Some students were unable to make up their minds and repeated numbers by listing more than one item as the #1 on their list.

FAMILIARITY WITH COMPUTERS

In order to get a sense of what students believe they will spend most of the time doing while working as translators, I asked them to list four statements from 1 through 4, according to what they considered the most relevant (#1) and the least relevant (#4) to their future routine.

WORKING WITH COMPUTERS	# 1	# 2	# 3	# 4	Totals
Researching different subjects	101	67	19	1	188
Networking with clients & colleagues	63	68	54	5	190
Comfortable with skills & knowledge	27	50	95	19	191
Dread sitting at the computer, isolated	5	4	19	162	190

Note: Some students were unable to make up their minds and repeated numbers by listing more than one item as the #1 on their list.

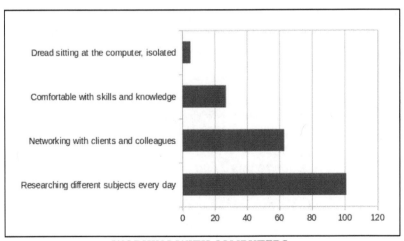

WORKING WITH COMPUTERS

As a general observation on student performance in class, there were a few issues with the first groups back in 2010, which have significantly improved throughout the years:

- **File Compression** — In one of our class assignments, I ask students to submit more than a file at once, thus requesting that they compress them. Providing a ZIP file (or RAR, if the case may be) is part of the exercise being graded, since this is a very common practice in the industry and they must learn how to do it. In the beginning, we had issues with students not being able to zip files correctly. Sometimes they would zip each file independently and then upload both to the online learning platform we use. Other times, they'd upload each file, then upload the two ZIPs together, and submit that resulting file. Since 2010, we've had fewer issues with unsuccessful or corrupted ZIPs, even though the zip-inside-a-zip issue still takes place frequently.

- **File Naming** — Hoping to prepare students for the "real world," I make sure they save their assignment files to their computer and learn how to rename them according to the guidelines set for the class. This will help them follow good file organization practices and make sure that the target language code is added at the end of a file name to make it easier for clients to identify their work. Since there are point deductions for deliveries that do not follow our file-naming guidelines, students have been increasingly better about paying attention to this detail.

- **Save Link As** — Depending on their settings, sometimes students click a link to an assignment file and their computer tries to open it with one of the programs it currently has installed. So, instead of clicking the file, I ask students to try to right-click it, so they can see a small menu with some options related to the link. That way they can save a copy directly to their computer. We still have some issues periodically, especially involving a couple of translation podcasts that are required material students must listen to before taking the week's quiz.

- **Leaving Comments on Documents** — During Week 7, we do a group exercise, in which a long news article (about 2,000 words) is selected and uploaded to Google Drive for the entire class to translate. In addition to strengthening their collaboration skills, this exercise also makes them feel more comfortable giving colleagues some feedback on their work by using the Comments tool, instead of making changes directly into the document. Even though it always starts out as a very stressful activity for those involved, 95% of students are grateful in the end and state that they learned valuable lessons while interacting with their classmates and working on a large-scale project.

- **Accents** — Because one of our course languages is Spanish, some students still have issues configuring their keyboards to add acute accents and tildes. Other difficult characters include long dashes (—), the euro sign (€), and the pound sign (£). In each occasion, tips are shared on how to create these characters using a combination of keys or the Insert > Symbol feature.

- **Double Space** — This is actually an entertaining conflict, because older students tend to leave two spaces after a period, which is a practice reminiscent of their days working with typewriters. I also used a manual typewriter back in the day, but have since adapted to electronic word processing rules. Whenever a student objects to this rule, I refer them to a funny article called *"Space Invaders."*[11]

---

[11] MANJOO Farhad. *Space Invaders*, Slate, January 12, 2011: http://bit.ly/T3-SpaceInvaders

SOCIAL NETWORKING

One of the marketing ideas we discuss in class is using social networking websites to build your presence online and advertise your services. In order to learn how students feel about it, I ask an open-ended question and let them express their likes and dislikes, marketing plans, hopes and fears. Here are the results of this survey:

INTEREST IN SOCIAL NETWORKING

Yes, I believe it's a valid marketing tool.	132
No, I'm not interested in social networking.	31
Maybe, I'm somewhat ambivalent about it.	15
TOTAL	178

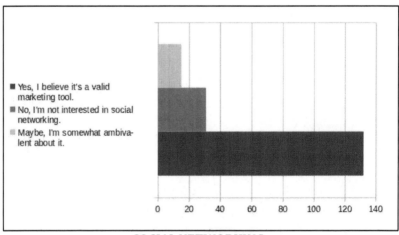

SOCIAL NETWORKING

As a general observation, I've noticed that reluctance to use social networking websites has decreased among students in this past four years, even though some are still skeptical whether the strategy would indeed work for business purposes.

Here are some of the stronger opposing opinions:

"I do not have the free time necessary to maintain an account."

"I've learned from other translators that they don't really get any work; it is more of a social thing."

"I really don't want any of my personal information to get into the wrong hands."

"Being a private person, getting responses from people who wanted to interact made me very uncomfortable."

"If I put myself out in the open then I'm subject to scams, identity theft, and just feel as if I give up my privacy."

"I am not at ease with its security features."

"I acknowledge the power of these sites, but I share neither my time nor my thoughts in that kind of media."

"They seem to be filled with a lot of trivial and useless things that would interfere with my efforts to project a more professional image."

"I'm not comfortable right now because I think I still need to learn and work on creating my business and to manage it properly before I get some clients."

"I feel that people overexpose themselves and it can be dangerous to put yourself out there too much. I know that sounds paranoid but it's how I feel."

"I'm awfully shy and have a problem 'selling' my skills. It's hard to promote yourself when there's no experience backing you up"

"I am not fond of this part of our new life style and it may be something to do with a generation issues."

"It's time consuming, however, and sometimes it feels like too much to handle if I don't practice good time management."

And here are some of the positive answers:

"If I was able to do that [get followers and likes] with a personal profile, I can't even imagine how beneficial it would be for my business"

"It's a great way to network and reach potential clients."

"I need to set up PROFESSIONAL profiles in order to keep business and personal life separate."

"It's a way to be open to everyone and show who you are."

"It makes sense that the more connections you have, the more easily you are found online."

"They're important forums to advance in this career."

"I can learn what people like or dislike about my business."

"You never know where a potential client is going to find you. It'll help me to generate more business."

"It is important to establish a professional persona that only barely intersects one's flesh-and-bone persona."

"We need to stay with the times and this includes taking advantage of the free resources available to us. At the same time, it makes me feel a little inadequate to see how busy others are posting while all I do is work... Hmmm..."

"It's almost impossible nowadays to avoid social media in order to spread the word about a business."

"I'd target the information to be specific to the 'translation side' of me."

"The web is a very powerful tool that can take a life of its own and be of great assistance."

"I am an educated and mature adult. I know what information is relevant if I were to set up profiles on social networking websites."

VOLUNTEERING

Following up on social networking use, I ask students whether they would consider volunteering their time to localize these websites into their target language. Here are the results of this survey:

VOLUNTEERING TO SOCIAL NETWORKS

No, I wouldn't consider doing it.	85
Yes, I'd be able to acquire experience.	50
Maybe, I'm somewhat ambivalent about it.	27
TOTAL	162

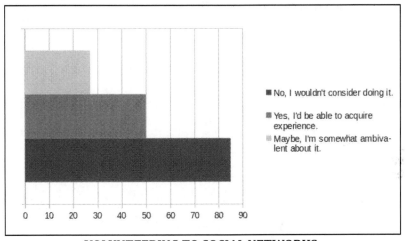

VOLUNTEERING TO SOCIAL NETWORKS

The comments students provided in this open ended question were split into, on the one hand, **concerns with crowdsourcing without compensation** and, on the other hand, **excitement about having an opportunity** to participate in the localization of a well-known website used worldwide.

Here are the reasons pointed out by those who were strongly opposed to the idea:

NO, I WOULDN'T CONSIDER IT	
They're for profit and should pay for translation services.	43
They're willing to use anyone with or without qualification; it diminishes our profession.	15
I want to be paid for my time and effort.	6
I dislike social networks.	5
I'm not comfortable with social networking and lack the proper terminology.	5
I don't want it to affect my reputation as a translator.	4
Complex projects shouldn't be divided among so many people.	3
I don't have lots of free time to donate.	3
It encourages crowdsourcing and could decrease opportunities for translators.	1
Not interested.	1
Because they have no oversight.	1

And here is what students who responded positively to the idea had to say:

YES, I'D BE ABLE TO ACQUIRE EXPERIENCE	
I'd acquire much-needed experience and have an opportunity to practice and get feedback.	26
It would be fun!	5
Users would benefit from it.	5
It would give me recognition for my work.	3
I'd be acquiring vocabulary.	2
If I'm available, why not?	2
If I got any perks (i.e. premium account for free).	2
But only to LinkedIn, because it's a professional site.	1
I'm interested in learning how social networks work.	1
I'd like to be a reviewer to correct other people's mistakes.	1
I'd be contributing to their improvement.	1

ONLINE JOB BOARDS

During our sixth week together, I ask students to visit some of the online job boards we discussed during our lesson, as well as others they may have found out about while doing their own research. As part of their homework, they must go through the process of creating an account, building a profile, and rating their experiences.

My main objective in having them work with it at this point is to allow them to **become familiar with the job board environment**, which is new to the vast majority of them, so they can see for themselves what's "out there." While completing the form made available by these sites, they have a chance to **reflect on the professional skills** they currently have and the ones they wish to develop. The information required by job boards will also **help them structure their resumes** better and highlight what they're good at doing.

The first obstacle some of them encounter is the idea that they must pay before they can go through with the process. While many job boards require a premium so members can enjoy the perks that come with a paid account, I reassure them that **they do not need to subscribe to a service** in order to have a free account and a basic profile.

Since most of them are still trying to establish themselves, in between jobs, or hoping to soon switch careers, I always tell them that **this is not the right time for them to invest money into job boards or software** before making the most of free accounts and trials. Their priority is to **become familiar, feel comfortable, and analyze** which options will indeed fit into their future or developing careers.

Yet another concern they have is **anxiety about sharing their information online**. This is sometimes a consequence of their **feeling too exposed** because they are either **very private individuals** or believe they're **not yet qualified or prepared** to have a professional profile up and running.

When students strongly react to having such minimal on-line presence, I let them know that they can delete their profiles once the class is over and encourage them to see it as just a school assignment. Odds are they won't be getting any private messages during the few remaining weeks of class, right after their information is entered onto the website. I remind them that **gaining exposure as a freelancer online is actually a long process** and there are gazillions of webpages online, so unless they are already using a job board profile as a professional marketing tool, people will hardly stumble upon their page by chance simply because it now exists on the web.

This exaggerated explanation seems to give them some sense of reality and make them feel better about the exercise. Having a job board profile, a webpage, a blog or a website is not the same as setting up a physical office, because there is no guarantee people will decide to walk in. These are only tools you can use to let potential clients know about you, but **you still have to do all the leg work yourself**.

For those who believe they're not "ready for primetime," so to speak, I remind them that **everybody has to start somewhere**. None of us jumped out of our mother's womb with several degrees and qualifications. However, if we're making a strong effort to improve ourselves, it's better to lay out a foundation and build it up as we take every small step towards growing professionally, rather than waiting to be ready and, only then, finally getting started.

Keep in mind that resumes, portfolios, and professional profiles are living beings, in that they'll grow and change the more experiences you acquire. If you start keeping track of what you do now, it'll only make things easier for you along the way.

Then there are other students who are **reluctant to disclose their info due to scammers** who may try to get a hold of their bank info or steal their identity.

This is a legitimate concern (See *Section 3* above.) As long as you **don't disclose the identifiers you usually use for financial transactions**—such as your social security, your mother's maiden name, and PINs or passwords to bank accounts or credit/debit cards—your finances will be safe.

As for identity theft, it is an unfortunate side effect of having an online presence, so you can opt to only send a copy of your resume when a potential client requests it, instead of attaching it to a job board profile.

All in all, students actually enjoy our Week 6 homework once they get past the initial discomfort. Going through job boards, with all its positives and negatives, is something that opens up a world to them.

Many have mentioned that they enjoyed reading what clients are looking for, so they have a **better idea of how to position themselves in the market**. Others liked going through profiles of translators with whom they share a similar background, so they are able to **set themselves goals** on how to improve their resume and experiences to **get a competitive edge**. And a few of them are happy to have this minimal presence online because they don't plan on creating a website or blog any time soon, so **having an internet address they can refer their clients to** is something that can really change their marketing perspectives.

And when it comes to using job boards as a business tool, students are asked to rate four tasks from 1 through 4, according to what they believe to be the most relevant (#1) and the least relevant (#4) to their activities.

Unsurprisingly, they are looking forward to resorting to job boards to **find job leads** (109), followed by **setting up profiles** (59), **interacting with colleagues** (21) and finding **educational opportunities** through webinars or software made available at a discounted price.

USING ONLINE JOB BOARDS	# 1	# 2	# 3	# 4	Totals
Applying for jobs	109	43	14	22	188
Setting up profiles	59	96	24	9	188
Forum to interact with colleagues	21	36	94	37	188
Education Opportunities	8	11	52	117	188

Note: Some students were unable to make up their minds and repeated numbers by listing more than one item as the #1 on their list.

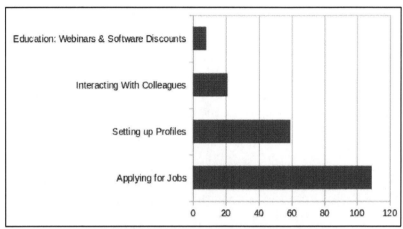

#1 PRIORITY WHEN USING JOB BOARDS

TRANSLATION TOOLS

During Weeks 8 and 9, it's time to talk about Computer-Assisted Translation (CAT) and machine translation—which is definitely the most anticipated part of our ten weeks together at Tools and Technology in Translation.

That's when we're able to explore these solutions in plain terms, as an introduction to what the technology can do for us, translators. Students are mostly mesmerized by the concept and eager to see it in action.

However, while putting the class together, we decided not to focus on one CAT in particular, since there would unfortunately be no time for anything else, but rather give students a notion of what these programs are capable of doing and how different they are from automated translation.

This way, students not only have a chance to learn more about what happens behind the scenes when a translation memory is being updated, but we also discuss matches, repetitions, and glossary management.

A few students (2%) had never heard about CATs before, either because they're brand new to the industry and are yet to get familiar with the terminology, or because they've been mostly working as interpreters and never needed to use translation tools.

With that in mind, one of the open-ended survey questions of the week was intended to determine how many of them had used a CAT, out of curiosity or professionally, and how many were willing to give it a try.

HAVE YOU EVER USED A CAT TOOL?

No, but I look forward to trying one.	159
Yes, I've used a CAT tool at some level.	19
Yes, I use it professionally quite often.	5
TOTAL	183

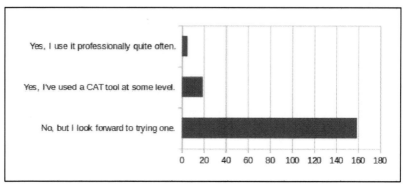

HAVE YOU EVER USED A CAT TOOL?

I intentionally asked an open-ended question so that students could volunteer their own impressions in terms of what they had experienced before the class. **Some students (15%) mentioned the reasons why they had not used CATs before**, and here is what they said:

I HAVEN' T USED A CAT YET BECAUSE...

Price	10
Not enough knowledge / lacking computer skills	6
This is the first time I've ever heard of it	4
Don't need it for the type of work I do	4
Not really interested in it	2
Only volunteering at the moment	1
I receive most material in PDF	1

The only student who was more strongly against translation technology seemed to have slightly mistaken CATs with automated translation when explaining why there was no interest in using such software:

"No, I think there is nothing like human translation because many CATs are very literal when translating and the flow of the documents is not natural."

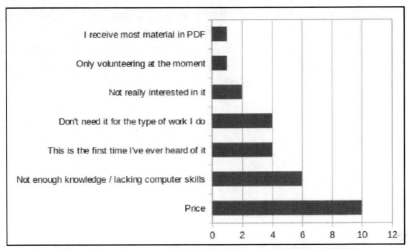

WHY HAVEN'T YOU EVER GIVEN A CAT TOOL A TRY?

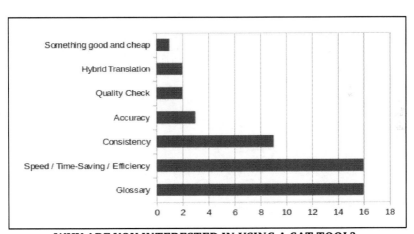

WHY ARE YOU INTERESTED IN USING A CAT TOOL?

Likewise, a few of them also volunteered their own impressions as far as what they expect to achieve once they incorporate a CAT into their routine as translators. **Some students (26%) mentioned the reasons why they would like to give this technology a try**:

I'M INTERESTED IN...

Glossary Management	16
Speed / Time-Saving / Efficiency	16
Consistency	9
Accuracy	3
Quality Check	2
Hybrid Translation	2
Something good and cheap	1

Other students (19%) disclosed specific information about which tools they had already installed and used at some point, either because they were "playing around with it to see what CATs are like" or because they've already implemented one of these tools into their regular work. Once again, the idea was to have them volunteer the name of tools they were familiar with, so no alternatives were given. For that reason, a few (3,8%) ended up mentioning software that would be more accurately classified as machine translation [I] or glossary management programs [II].

I HAVE ALREADY USED...

Trados	7
Wordfast	5
Swordfish	5
Google Translate [I]	4
OmegaT	3
Across	3
memoQ	2
Babylon [II]	2
DejaVu	1
Google Translator Toolkit	1
SEER (SEER English Spanish Translator) [II]	1
My own tool in Excel [II]	1

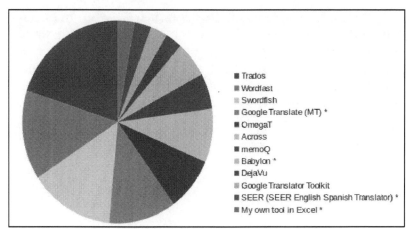

WHICH CAT TOOLS HAVE YOU EVER USED?

* Note: Some students mistook these tools for CATs

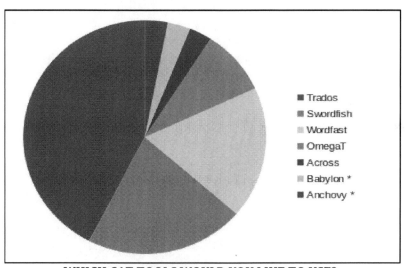

WHICH CAT TOOLS WOULD YOU LIKE TO USE?

* Note: Some students mistook these tools for CATs

For full-color charts, visit http://www.RafaLombardino.com/tools

The same is true about **students (18%) who mentioned which tools they would like to try** because they had already heard something positive from other translators or found information online during their own research. A few (1%) ended up mentioning software that would be more accurately classified as glossaries [I] or glossary management solutions [II].

I WOULD LIKE TO USE...

Trados	14
Swordfish	7
Wordfast	6
OmegaT	3
Across	1
Babylon [I]	1
Anchovy [II]	1

Moving on to a more general question, I asked them to express their opinions about translation tools, including CATs and machine translation (MT). More specifically, I asked them how useful they think translation technology is and what pros and cons they saw in using it.

A few students ended up answering both ways, often referring to CATs as very useful and MTs as a distraction. Consequently, their answers were tabulated in both categories.

Going through their answers about the positive and negative aspects of translation tools, I was able to compile a list and better analyze their concerns and excitement about working with programs that can assist them in their daily work.

WHAT IS YOUR OPINION ABOUT TRANSLATION TOOLS?

They are very useful.	152
I'm not sure yet.	22
They are an unreliable distraction.	8
TOTAL	182

Better productivity and higher efficiency—such a time saver! _____ 67
Automating repeated work and
  incorporating past translations into current projects _____ 37
More consistency and accuracy / Quality assurance capabilities _____ 34
Terminology management / Glossaries _____ 21
Word count log to plan our progress and offer discounts _____ 13
More job opportunities—it's a competitive edge _____ 3
Convenience; no need to reinventing the wheel with each translation _____ 2
The faster you translate, the more money you make _____ 2
Retrieving immediate answers at the vocabulary level _____ 2
I'll feel more confident and professional;
  technology empowers translators! _____ 2

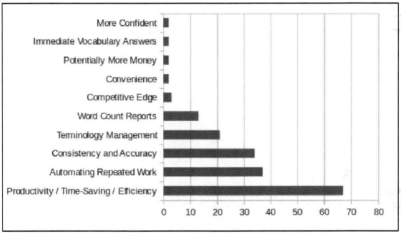

PROS OF WORKING WITH TRANSLATION TECHNOLOGY

Here's how one student is already planning on using CAT tools in a professional setting:

> *"No, I have not yet tried any CAT tools, but I am excited to try one. In my volunteer translations for Kiva, I know there is a lot of repetitive language and I can definitely see how a CAT tool could speed up my work and improve my consistency."*

NEGATIVE SIDE EFFECTS OF WORKING WITH TRANSLATION PROGRAMS
Relying too much on technology and
 not knowing how to work without it _____ 14
Expensive initial investment _____ 14
Steep learning curve—CATs look intimidating! _____ 10
Not applicable to literary translations _____ 8
Technology improvement could make this a human-free industry _____ 4
Technology doesn't make you a better translator _____ 3
Technology promotes the mechanization
 of translated text and loss language nuances _____ 3
Technology may create unrealistic expectations from clients _____ 2
Technology is great, but it doesn't have common sense _____ 1
Building a database is time consuming _____ 1
It's hard to collaborate remotely and in real time _____ 1

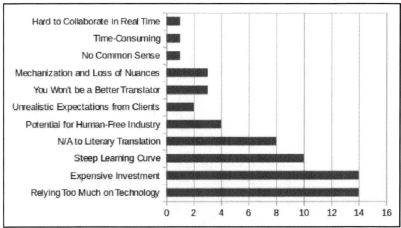

CONS OF WORKING WITH TRANSLATION TECHNOLOGY

A student who voiced a negative opinion towards machine translations more strongly had the following to say:

> *"Using MT not only worships mediocrity because it has neither coherence nor accuracy, but it is also very harmful to communication and therefore contributes to backwardness."*

Some students voiced their opinion about MT specifically and their impressions are highlighted below.

WAYS WORKING WITH MACHINE TRANSLATION WOULD HELP ME
Minimizing "thinking time"—quick reference
    to get a gist of the source text _____ 24
Useful if editing is not too extensive _____ 7
Good research solution _____ 2
I'd like to try a hybrid CAT+MT solution _____ 2

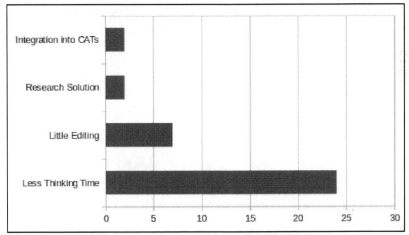

PROS OF USING MACHINE TRANSLATION

WHY I DISAPPROVE OF MACHINE TRANSLATIONS
People assume results are final, but humans
    are the brains behind a translation _____ 18
Lack of context for word choices—too literal _____ 15
Not an asset to my professional life _____ 14
Post-editing machine translation is time consuming and demanding _____ 14
Not a clear, reliable overall picture—very limited capabilities _____ 8
Lack of cultural sensitivity _____ 2
MTs do more harm than good _____ 1

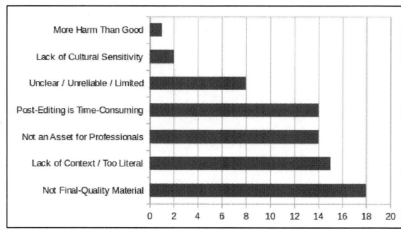

CONS OF USING MACHINE TRANSLATION

Here are some of the negative comments students made about MT specifically:

> *"MTs are not useful at all and would not help me in my daily professional life. Contrarily, it would be a waste of my time."*

> *"No human interfacing—it's 100% done by computers."*

> *"Literal translation; word per word: loss of meaning."*

> *"There is no distinction between female and male nouns."*

> *"It's an unprofessional approach and an insult to speakers of the target language."*

> *"MTs undermine the role of the translator."*

> *"Great deal of liability involved in connection with a business and its reputation."*

> *"Compared to CATs, I cannot record my progress into a database, so I don't know what else there is to translate— MTs will not indicate any repetitions."*

CONCLUSION

After analyzing all this data, we can conclude that translation students **value their current language and business knowledge**, and believe it will contribute to their future activities. They highlighted their **appreciation for languages,** as well as their **writing, grammar, and reading skills** as important assets to their career as translators and interpreters, and have identified their **sense of organization and people skills**, as well as their **eagerness to learn** as crucial elements to developing their own business.

As beginners in the T&I industry, they know that they still have to **strengthen their business and technology skills** in order to get a competitive edge and develop a sustainable operation. Although they stated they were already organized, they wanted to learn more about **developing their business organization skills,** and then **incorporate social media and networking to their public relations efforts**, in addition to finding their average output (as in words per hour or day) and identifying a potential **specialization**. As for the technology aspect, they want to learn more about **CAT Tools**, strengthen their overall **computer skills**, and find **researching tools** they can incorporate into their professional lives.

In regards to their activities as potential telecommuting professionals, they indicated that they are **eager to research different subjects** with each new project and to **network with clients and colleagues over the internet**. Watching these groups for the past four years, I can say that the number of cases in which students express **frustration with routine computer issues has decreased**, and they have been increasingly able to resolve day-to-day problems on their own, such as **fixing keyboard settings** and **creating zip files**.

When it comes to advertising their services online, the vast **majority confirmed that they feel comfortable resorting to social networking and job boards**, even though the **minority**

expressed their strong disapproval of such strategies. That is also confirmed by the fact that **most students would not consider volunteering their time to localizing large websites**, including social network platforms, and **would rather donate their time** as translators and interpreters **to causes they really believe in**.

And, about the use of job boards, **most students were excited** to have an opportunity to create a professional profile during class exercises, and only **a few expressed their anxiety** due to being insecure and unsure about their current abilities, or **fear of being "too exposed"** once they created a page with their professional information.

Now, considering what is undoubtedly the most anticipated part of our ten-weeks together, **the overwhelming majority of students said they have never had a chance to work with CAT tools, but are certainly looking forward to** trying them out. They mostly haven't had the opportunity **due to the high investment** it represents and their **lack of knowledge** to do so, but are **interested in the glossary feature** and the potential to **increase their efficiency**.

Finally, when **reflecting on how technology can help** translators advance their career, they mentioned **higher productivity, automated repeated work, and more consistency** and the main benefits, and **becoming too dependent on technology, making a high investment** and **facing steep learning curve** as the downsides of implementing these technologies into their daily professional lives.

EPILOGUE

Now that we have reached the end of this book, I'd like to invite you to look back at what your thoughts were before you started reading it.

I'd like to ask the following questions to **future translators and interpreters**:

- Did your ideas on the T&I industry change that much?
- Or did you already have a clear picture of the ups and downs of this interesting, but deeply challenging industry?
- Do you realize now that technology will definitely play an important part in your life?
- Or did you already feel pretty comfortable with your computer skills and are glad you'll be able to put them to good use as a language professional?

Start thinking about your point of view and how it has changed, if it did change at all. Reflect on the aspects that make you feel comfortable during your daily professional tasks and what may become an issue.

Write it all down and try to be as specific as possible, because this is something that will most likely help you to prepare for the real-world out there and become part of your business plan. This way, you will have a clearer picture of your own strengths and weaknesses, then use your time to balance things out.

Now I'd like to ask the following questions to **current translation and interpreting instructors**:

- Does the profile of beginning language professionals shown here match your experiences?
- How are your students responding to T&I technology?
- What can you do to help them expand their horizons on the subject?
- How could you prepare them better for the road ahead?

RECOMMENDED READING

The Importance of Specialization in the Field of Translation

By Gina Bushnell

I started my first attempts in the amazing and intricate field of translation working as an engineer, not as a professional translator per se, when I had to edit a thick manual translated from English to Spanish for a conference on aseptic technology, which I was in charge of at the time.

Although this is not the "usual path" to becoming a professional translator—that is, having studied first to become a translator and then specializing in a translation subject—this is one of the paths taken by many colleagues in the technical field. Why, you may ask? Because the need to know and use specific vocabulary correctly, as required in that field, is of utmost importance to communicate effectively. Hence, the necessity and the practicality of specializing in a translation field when you want to become a professional and successful translator.

However, this is a point that sometimes is overlooked or hard to understand for the novice translator and for some of my students in the introductory courses that I teach at UCSD Extension. Sometimes it is due to the wrong idea that it is easy to find more translation jobs, or make more money, if you translate everything that comes your way.

What about the time involved not only in researching the vocabulary but also in understanding the subjects with which you are not familiar? "You cannot translate what you don't understand," I always stress to my students. And what about the quality that you are ethically bound to deliver to your customer?

If you do not have a specialty field yet, start studying and researching a subject that interests you. Do you like the medical field, the legal field, or perhaps any subdivisions of the technical field, like pulse power technology?

Remember, it is always easier and better to translate in a field you know well. If you want to be a successful translator, you cannot afford to deliver poor quality translations. How are you going to find future customers if you cannot keep the first ones who hire you for your translation services?

GEORGINA BUSHNELL, B.S. in Food Engineering with graduate studies in Dairy Science and Technology in Sweden and Great Britain. A native Spanish speaker from Mexico City, Georgina has over 10 years' experience internationally in food quality control and over 18 years' experience translating and interpreting in scientific and technical fields. She has been teaching at UCSD Extension since 2001 and has also been a guest speaker at UCSD Career Services, *Asociación de Traductores e Intérpretes Profesionales de Baja California*, Interpreter Services Department of the U.S. District Court in San Diego, and Riverside County Office of Education.

RECOMMENDED READING

No Pain, No Gain: On Finding Direct Clients

By Judy Jenner

Newcomers to the profession—actually, everyone in the profession—must, at some point, decide if they want to work for themselves or look for an in-house translator/interpreter position. Especially here in the United States, these in-house positions are very far and few between, so the vast majority of linguists end up working for themselves, which means that they run small businesses, many times a one-person businesses.

Now, the next decision is whether to try to work with language services providers (LSPs), also known as translation/interpreting agencies among other terms, or whether to work with direct clients. This arrangement is usually more lucrative for the linguist, as there's no person in the middle taking his or her cut of the earnings, and typically results in more direct communication and oftentimes better working conditions.

As a matter of course, linguists can work for both agencies and direct clients, but by speaking at conferences around the country and the world, I've noticed that many colleagues prefer to work with direct clients, but don't know how to go about finding them. The following is based on my experience running a boutique translation and interpreting service that works exclusively with direct clients.

- **Finding direct clients can be relatively challenging.** If it were easy, everyone would do it. The reason it's great to work with agencies is that they essentially do all the marketing and sales and pass the contract on to you. When you try to find direct clients, you are the Marketing and Sales Department, and not everyone enjoys that. Before you start thinking about working with direct clients, ask yourself: "Am I comfortable doing sales and business development?"

- **Spread the word.** Business development is akin to politics in the sense that the more people know you, the more likely you are to get business or get elected. You can be the world's greatest translator and/or interpreter, but if no one knows you exist, it doesn't do you any good. Start spreading the word and attend networking events, get-togethers organized by local business associations, and tell all your friends about your new business. Your friends have jobs and connections, and they might know others who need your services.

- **Get out of your comfort zone.** No one likes receiving cold calls or cold e-mails, so I strongly suggest staying away from that strategy. Rather, research your industries and reach out to key people through connections, perhaps on LinkedIn. Attend the events that your target audience attends. For instance, if you are a medical interpreter, you might want to attend a conference for diversity in health care and see if you can make some connections there. Walking into a room full of people you don't know is intimidating, but don't be overwhelmed: focus on making just one contact.

- **There are really only two ways to market your services: online and offline**, and I suggest a combination of both. Online (building a brand, blogging, being active on Twitter, LinkedIn, etc.) is quick and painless, but there's no substitute for human interaction, so I recommend attending one in-person event a week (or a month; whatever works).

- **Be prepared without being pushy.** You don't want to shove your business card into new acquaintances' hands. Rather, be natural, come prepared with interesting small talk, and ask questions about the other person and their work. Make sure you can talk intelligently about your business when asked and bring plenty of business cards.

- **You never know where your next client will come from.** My business partner met one of our loveliest clients at a yoga studio (the client was the yoga instructor!)

Best of luck on your journey!

JUDY JENNER is a master-level court-certified Spanish interpreter in Nevada, a court-certified interpreter in California, and an experienced legal, marketing and e-commerce translator with clients on three continents. She runs a successful small translation and interpreting business, Twin Translations, with her twin sister, Dagmar. They are the authors of a book on translation, *The Entrepreneurial Linguist: The Business-School Approach to Freelance Translation*, which has sold more than 3,000 copies and is required reading at universities around the world. Judy is the former president of the Nevada Interpreters and Translators Association and is a columnist for the American Translators Association's Chronicle. Judy and Dagmar blog about translation, interpretation, and the business of translation on the award-winning blog, *Translation Times*. Judy is a frequent keynote speaker at translation and interpretation conferences, and has given workshops in ten countries. Judy was born in Austria, grew up in Mexico City, and has lived in the United States since she was a teenager. She lives in Las Vegas, NV.

RECOMMENDED READING

Interpreting? I can do that!

By Jennifer De La Cruz

Over the course of my career as an interpreter trainer, when I would ask students brand new to the field why they became interested, every semester the majority of them had the same story: they grew up speaking two languages, being the family bilingual aid, and thought that being a professional interpreter would be the logical career choice. Their expectations were high, both of the class and of themselves, and by the time the first quiz rolled around, their eyes were wide and jaws dropped: they had their work cut out for them!

The program I worked with for ten years had only the prerequisite of self-declared near-native fluency in our working languages. This was a great opportunity for many who wanted to explore the field but could not get into more rigorous programs, or needed to continue working their day jobs and study in the evenings. Although every term I had students from across the spectrum in skills and experience, the common thread was that many came in with the misconception that conversational skills in a language are sufficient. They had plenty of experience speaking both languages, they had familiarity with cultural differences, but they usually lacked more than just the vocabulary and ethics. They were now expected to think critically about every word they used, its shades of meaning, implications, and overall correctness when using somebody else's words and thoughts—all a first for many.

Although our program was clearly represented as introductory, the biggest misconception was that it was guaranteed to prepare them to work as a certified interpreter in the courts, at hospitals, and for businesses, and that potential employers would see their education with us as proof-positive that they were the right person for the job.

Students were usually surprised to learn that not only might they have to take additional courses to improve their language skills, but they would likely be tested further before they would get an interpreter position. For those thinking about working for entities that didn't require formal certification, we instructors knew that the competition would be tough, and that they may have to work more on their game—sometimes a lot more—before expecting conversational skills to turn into interpreter quality. As a vocational program, we catered to students who were looking to change careers, so the extra time and study required often came as a bit of a shock.

Unlike the field of translation, interpretation requires professionals to have excellent pronunciation and speed in both their A and B languages. There were students who came to class with speech impediments or with extensive knowledge but a bit slow in rendering, and they soon discovered that the field of translation could be a better fit. There, not only would they avoid the spoken skills problems, they could also dodge the issue of having to be a lightning-fast thinker and speaker.

As their instructors, we always aimed in our program to think of options for their future professional careers, considering the whole student and job market realities. We prided ourselves in being more than a clearinghouse for test skills and strategies; our focus was on meeting the students where they were, inspiring and informing them to join the quest to best bridge communication gaps in our society.

Interpreting students are a social bunch, often coming in with the expectation that their spoken language skills are meant as a gift they can use to help others. Although I always reminded them that, depending on the industry they chose, they might want to consider interpreting for the love of language first and foremost, the spirit of openness was always present. This allowed us to take the misconceptions about themselves and about our program and turn them into a vector for thinking about their future in the language industry.

Keeping in mind the entry requirements of the interpreting program one chooses to work with, instructors are smart to keep common misconceptions in mind and to create a learning environment that allows enough flexibility to tailor lesson plans to the students both individually and as a group. Finally, as an instructor, keep your own expectations in check. Set the bar high, but know that it isn't all about perfection on quizzes and exams; in vocational training, our views about every aspect of our field are called upon to guide and mentor far beyond any glossary.

JENNIFER DE LA CRUZ is certified as a Spanish/English interpreter by the Administrative Office of the U.S. Courts and the Judicial Council of California, and as a translator by the American Translators Association (Spanish to English and English to Spanish). She holds a Bachelor's degree in Spanish, and has taught interpreting and translation during most of her career. After spending nearly a decade as a medical interpreter, she joined the Superior Courts of California as a staff interpreter and continues working as a freelance translator. She is an adjunct instructor for the UCSD Extension Translation Program and sits on the Board of Directors of NAJIT.

RECOMMENDED READING

Why I Use a CAT Tool to Translate Books

By Rafa Lombardino

Computer-Assisted Translation—that's what CAT stands for. If you're not in the translation business, or if you're in the book translation business, odds are you're not familiar with the concept. No, CATs don't do the work themselves; we still need humans to translate documents (and books) from one language into another because a machine-powered translation doesn't have "gut feelings" or "cultural sensitivity." Machine translation just won't cut it, but that's another story...

What this translation technology does is keep track of what translators type. Each sentence of the source document is isolated, so a translator can type the respective translation and the combination is saved to a database. This is very useful when we translate technical materials and have been working with the same client for a long time, because there is a great chance that you'll come across sentences that are 100% identical or a close match to something you've translated in the past. So, in other words, CATs work as your memory and you don't have to remember or look through old files to make sure you're using the same words you did in the past.

Well, why am I talking about it on a blog dedicated to book translations? The sentences in a book will hardly repeat themselves, right? Wrong! I've recently had such an experience and it shows how valuable CAT tools can be. When I was translating Beto Córdova's "The Alliance," there were many repetitions that called for this technology, considering a book with character-centered chapters that have distinctive voices in each one of them, as well as lots of internal monologues and flashbacks, so it was only natural that key sentences were reinforced throughout the story.

In general, once you load a document into a CAT tool, you can see the original sentence on the left-hand side or top of the translation screen and then you can type the translation on the right-hand side or the bottom of the screen. This translation unit (language A + language B) is then recorded into a database and, once that sentence or something similar shows up again, the CAT retrieves the recorded translation unit for you and you can choose to use the exact same translation or adapt it according to the changes in the new original sentence.

Besides that, CATs can also be useful for glossary management. Some books will have keywords that you'll need to use over and over. Maybe a character uses certain lingo and you want to be true to that by using the same equivalents and register in the translation, so it's important to keep the vocabulary consistent. The easiest way to do it is using a CAT.

While you're translating a sentence, you can highlight a word or expression in the source and highlight the corresponding terms in the translation, then save it to a database called "glossary" or "termbase." Having the CAT display relevant words already added to your glossary, depending on the sentence you're currently translating, really beats spreadsheet-style glossaries, because you don't have to stop and look through it alphabetically, as you would a dictionary, to find the word you're looking for. And, believe me, that saves a lot of time and effort, while keeping consistency.

The CAT I've been using since 2008 is called Swordfish and I've selected it because we run Linux computers in the office, and this is one of the very few tools that actually works in any operating system—no need for emulators.

It also gives me the advantage of working on either my desktop or laptop, because I only have to disable the license in one and enable it in the other to pick it up right where I've left it off. And it's compatible with other tools, too, so I can collaborate with clients and colleagues who use other solutions without major complications.

If you're a translator and haven't tried out a CAT tool yet, I highly recommended that you take advantage of 30-day free trials to get an idea of what they're all about—whether you're translating technical documents or books. I'm sure a CAT will come in handy.

Originally posted at
http://bit.ly/T3-CAT-and-Books

RECOMMENDED READING

A Perspective From a Literary Translator

By Rafa Lombardino

When people think about translators, they usually picture someone in a conference booth, listening to a speech on the headphones in one language and speaking softly into a microphone in another language. Then you explain these are interpreters, and what you do is translate written words. Upon hearing that, they immediately transport their stereotype to a trendy cafe and imagine you typing a book translation away on a cool-looking laptop while sipping a latte.

While I know there are people out there who match the profile, it would be very hard for me to work in public like that. I don't know about you, but I sure am not the only one who has to act out some expressions in order to translate them correctly, because looking it up in the dictionary simply wouldn't be enough.

How many times have I found myself nodding, shrugging, frowning, taking a deep breath, clicking my tongue, climbing a hill, throwing a knife, slashing someone's heel... I've even given my kids a fright a couple of times, going from quietly typing to suddenly making weird moves and noises.

Then there was this time while I was translating the last quarter of John O'Dowd's *Mahko's Knife*. The author mentioned someone's "hollow of the neck." I immediately touched the hollow of my neck with my index finger and the word "saboneteira" came to mind. Literally, it's a "soap dish" in Brazilian Portuguese. However, I wasn't sure the term would apply to the male anatomy as well, as described in the book.

I looked up the expression, combined with the word "male" in Google Images. Results in English confirmed that it was indeed the area right below the Adam's apple. In Portuguese, however, results for "saboneteira * homem" or "saboneteira * masculino" were completely unrelated and, sometimes, of the X-rate kind... I then looked for "pomo de Adão" (literally, "Adam's apple") to see if maybe scientific images would give me some anatomy knowledge. Again, it was no use.

The next best thing I had was a live male specimen, aka "my husband." He was lying down on the couch, watching TV, when I knelled beside him and reached for his Adam's apple. "What you doing?" he asked. "Shhh! Don't talk!" I replied briskly. Yes, living with a translator can be romantic like that sometimes...

Suddenly, the inspiration came to me. "Thanks, honey!" I said, as I got up quickly to return to my laptop before the solution escaped me, leaving him there with that what-just-happened look on his face. And that is how I happily settled for *espaço côncavo logo abaixo do pomo de Adão*, literally "that concave space right below the Adam's apple."

If you allow me one last graphic analogy, I'd say that, from my point of view, working as a translator—be it with technical or literary materials—is pretty much like a tampon commercial. You know, we always see those women smiling on the ads, ready to go play tennis or take a stroll at the beach, but if you're a woman in your fertile years, you know pretty well that there's nothing to smile about and you just have to go through the pain and the inconvenience until you come out on the other side of it.

So, next time you think of translators, keep in mind all the struggle we have to go through to find the right words and put them to paper. Our work is not about replacing words like a walking dictionary; it's about powering through the cramps and headaches until your work is done. Then, and only then, you're allowed to put that silly smile on your face.

Originally posted at
http://bit.ly/T3-LiteraryPerspective

RECOMMENDED READING

Literature in Gaming Translation

By Rafa Lombardino

I must confess: My knowledge of Greek mythology is very limited. I know the standard information we learn by osmosis, with clearer images borrowed from movies. I just never imagined I would need a deeper understanding on the subject to work on gaming translations.

The other day I received a two-column document containing the original in English on the left and a blank column on the right where I should input my translation.

I started reading through the document and was fascinated by the rich information on Poseidon and Hades, two gods who were Zeus' brothers. That was the setup for *God of War*, a successful gaming franchise, and I was now going to fill in some blanks and translate part of the back story about the main characters and their army of loyal warriors.

The images that immediately came to mind were those from blockbuster movies, such as *Clash of the Titans*, *Immortals*, and *Percy Jackson & The Olympians: The Lightning Thief*. Unfortunately, I haven't spent as much time in this ancient world to have all the information pouring out of me during the translation process, so some research was required.

And, while I was translating just that little bit of text, which is obviously part of a much larger context within the game, it got me thinking: How large is a complete game translation project of this magnitude and how many translators are involved in it? As in any assignment of this nature, there has to be some sense of writing style, so gamers don't feel awkward bouncing between narratives that are told in very different voices.

And how about terminology consistency? I've researched how key terms have been depicted in literature in Brazilian Portuguese, my target language. But what if another translator didn't go through the trouble to translate Scylla as "Cila" and Charybdis as "Caríbdis"?

While looking up more information about large-scale gaming translations, I came across this: "An Atari localization meltdown over Neverwinter Nights' 1.2 million words, and how some fan translations made it into Baldur's Gate Enhanced Edition, beating out professional contractors." Yes, fans are passionate about the games they play and most likely are the ones who know all the ins and outs of each level, sometimes maybe better than some developers themselves. But I was really curious about how accurate and consistent fan translations can really be.

Another article I came across talked about how *World of Warcraft* reached Brazil in 2011 after a Herculean localization process by gaming company Blizzard. It got great reviews, one of which summarized how I feel about it:

"When we have the story, features and aspects of a game told in our native language, we can learn new elements that used to go unnoticed before. Beyond that, language is the most important cultural mechanism in a country. When people have the ability to communicate through a common language, they exchange more than information: Notions of identity, nation, and the collective are then created."

I wish I could take a larger role in the *God of War* translation, so I wouldn't feel like just another piece of a puzzle and have actually made a significant contribution to create this sense of identity in the target country. Unfortunately, it's out of my control and the only thing I can do about it is go read some book on Greek mythology. And also watch *Wrath of the Titans*, which has been waiting for me for a couple of months...

RECOMMENDED READING

A "10% Off" Tag on
Knowledge and Accountability?

By Rafa Lombardino

Would you go to a lawyer's office and say, "Hey, if I bring coffee and donuts to our meeting, could you drop your price down from $250 per hour to $175?"

You would never consider that, would you? Lawyers offer specialized knowledge of the law, help you navigate through legal troubles, and contribute to your business success. So why should translators be treated any differently?

Since we don't necessarily need a degree or license to work as translators, many tend to believe that translating is an informal occupation, a side job we can do in our spare time, you know, while we're taking a break from our "real job."

I can assure you that is not the case for most professional translators, at least not in the long run. I started as a translator back in 1997, while I was teaching English as a second language. However, after translation work put me through college, I decided to make it official and become a full-time translator, starting my own business and teaming up with like-minded professionals whose main purpose is to offer responsible language services.

"Responsible services?" you might ask. Being the go-between, transmitting somebody else's thoughts and intentions in a different language, does come with a lot of responsibility.

Just as a lawyer represents you in court and before authorities, translators and interpreters represent you in your interactions with a target audience that doesn't speak your language. Translators can make or break a project, contributing to having consumers either rush to the store to buy your product or laugh at your expense.

With that in mind, I'd like to go straight to the point: Why do clients feel the need to ask for discounts when hiring translation services? Here are the Top 3 arguments I've heard in the past few years:

"The text is very short!" — Translating is not about word count alone; it's about content and context. Taking an example from David Bellos' book *Is That a Fish in your Ear?*, the following headline is pretty short, but it takes considerable effort to be rendered in an intelligible way in another language and culture: "GOP VEEP PICK ROILS DEMS". Anyone hired to translate these five little words must first know about American politics and be up to date on current events to produce something that can be understood by non-US readers.

"The text is very easy!" — Information on sophisticated chemical processes is commonplace for chemical engineers. An article on advances in cardiovascular surgery is very accessible to most physicians. Building codes and regulations are right up a civil engineer's or an architect's alley. However, specialization is just one of the aspects that go into translation. What may seem easy in the source language might not be easily transferred to the target language. Do the same technologies exist in the target country? What are the terms and concepts being used nowadays in that market pertaining to the specific area? Is there any cultural sensitivity that needs to be factored in? Even the simplest texts take research and tact to sound natural to readers in another language.

"If you give me a discount, I'll assign more work to you in the near future!" — Ah, the good old "volume discount"... More work simply means MORE WORK, period. If you go to a dental hygienist once every quarter, it means you like the service. Any dental hygienist would surely appreciate your loyalty, but they can't offer you free sessions if you promise to come back periodically. If they did that, they would soon be out of business. The same is true for translators: If we give discounts for a small project on the promise that more work will come our way or—worse—discounts for a huge project because you think long-term commitment provides us with some sort of financial stability, we'll be making less and less per hour and our bills simply won't pay for themselves.

When we name our rate per word, page, hour or project, a lot goes into that calculation. Most professional translators have a pretty good idea about our daily output in the best- and worst-case scenarios. When we first take a look at your files, we can estimate how long it will take us to finish the job and how much it is worth, considering our background, specialization, and other important variables, which also include our own expenses in getting the job done well.

We spend years studying and investing in our continuing education and the fruits of that investment go into every single project we accept. We also spend a lot of time learning about new technology, which will make our work more manageable on several fronts, from easy accessibility to legacy material through redundant backup solutions (CDs, zip drives, and servers in the cloud) all the way to the consistency provided by computer-assisted translation tools (which record our progress and allow us to retrieve previously translated sentences and refer to glossaries we've built with preferred terminology.)

Our investments actually "translate" into the time savings that we pass on to you when taking less time to get your project done correctly, while being more efficient and accurate in the process. And all that comes with a fair price tag.

Originally posted at
Bianca Bold's blog
Translation Client Zone
http://bit.ly/TCZ-130115
(AUDIO AVAILABLE)

RECOMMENDED READING

3 Ideas to Avoid Boredom and Stress

By Rafa Lombardino

Working on multiple projects is a big challenge. Each item needs your undivided attention so you'll meet your deadlines, achieve your goals, and keep clients happy. But you can only work for so long before you run out of steam, right? And, even if you have a flexible deadline, the smallest disruptions can bring about chaos. Here are 3 ideas to manage your boredom, meet your expectations, and get all projects done on time without giving in to stress or finding a way to procrastinate.

1.   Follow your schedule and rotate different tasks around

First of all, you gotta organize yourself! You can use a daily planner, a whiteboard, or an online calendar, but PLEASE plan your day beforehand to avoid any headaches. For example, I work with multiple translation projects and, besides completing my own translations, I also supervise colleagues who translate the same documents into their own language. If we didn't use a scheduling system, it would sure be a disaster—that means, missed deadlines and unhappy clients.

So, Step 1 is setting up the slots of time you'll dedicate to each project. If it's something short and simple, it'll be over before you need to take a break and move on to the next task. But if it's a larger project you're dealing with—let's say, a 10,000-word corporate sustainability report that is only due next week—plan yourself to dedicate a couple of hours to it here and there, intertwined with some much-needed downtime and tasks of a different nature to give your brain a break and still meet the deadline.

Using this 10,000-word translation as an example, one way to approach it is to schedule a couple of hours in the morning to get it started, take a quick break when the time is up (go get some coffee/tea/juice) and then do some unrelated task for the next half an hour or so (managing social media posts, writing a blog entry, answering emails, making phone calls...) Go back to the translation project for another hour and you'll most likely get a boost of productivity and work more easily on it, since it's now familiar to you, while still making progress on your to-do list and keeping your productivity up before it's time for lunch.

Even if you still do the same kind of task, but use a different approach, you're already allowing your brain to switch gears, restart and keep going for longer without getting tired. For instance, let's say I'm translating a long Portuguese-to-English document, so I take a break from it after a couple of hours and fit in a small English-to-Portuguese task to reboot. Otherwise, I run the risk of hitting a roadblock—my brain gets stuck—and my productivity drops.

THE KEY HERE IS TO STAY ORGANIZED and let all the pieces of the puzzle fall in the right place to make your tight schedule work. Still, don't overschedule yourself and leave room for unforeseen circumstances. Few things are worth stressing about and, sometimes, it's better to just take a quick break.

2.   Find your ideal "attention buffer"

Have you ever suffered from the Watching-the-Clock Syndrome? I guess everybody has, at one time or another. It's not that you dislike the task you're working on in that particular moment—okay, sometimes you keep at something for way too long and end up getting bored! It's usually just a matter of feeling that you're not making enough progress. Sometimes you think you should have written/translated/compiled X pages and you feel like you're trapped in quicksand and not moving forward at all.

Well, besides the "take a break and switch gears" approach mentioned above, there's one trick you could try: Implement an "attention buffer!" What I mean by that is simply something that will keep one of your senses preoccupied, providing some sort of time reference, so you don't feel you're lagging behind.

Some people think it's about multitasking and are completely against having any of their senses connected to something other than the task at hand, but what I'm actually talking about here is just allowing your brain to have some sort of an escape, so you don't get tired fast.

I'll explain: if I'm translating a document from Spanish to Portuguese, I like having some Brazilian music playing in the background—especially if it's Wednesday and I get to enjoy the 100% Brazilian mix that Lumen FM plays that day of the week. (And, before you ask me, yes, we speak Portuguese in Brazil...[12])

Listening to something in the language I'm writing in or translating to/from actually helps me relax and stay focused at the same time. Had I been listening to English or Italian while working on the Spanish/Portuguese language combo, then it'd certainly be a distraction! Sometimes, when I switch to an English-related task, having an NPR interview, a TV show, or a movie in the background actually works as motivation to get more mundane tasks done, including project management, scheduling, invoicing, etc.

It also works when I'm eventually stuck on a translation task and, I have to say, more than once Jon Stewart[13] and Stephen Colbert[14] have actually helped me find the perfect word I was looking for while eloquently making their point across in some of their seriously hilarious reports. You might not have realized it, but these two and their writing staff are true word nerds. Talk about serendipity!

---

[12] _____. *Why do Brazilians Speak Portuguese?* Transparent Language, August 15, 2007: http://bit.ly/T3-SpeakPortuguese
[13] http://bit.ly/T3-Wiki-TheDailyShow
[14] http://bit.ly/T3-Wiki-TheColbertReport

All I know is that, if I have absolute silence while working, I actually feel uncomfortable and restless, as if I weren't making much progress on my tasks (30 minutes end up feeling like 3 hours!) and I soon get tired, distracted, and frustrated.

However, there are always exceptions, of course. I usually can't have much going on in the background if I'm translating a novel, for example, because I need to be completely immersed in the universe that the author has created, as if I could see, hear, smell, taste, and touch everything that the characters are experiencing. So, in that case, music is indeed a distraction—unless it's a soundtrack mentioned by the author in connection to characters and events.

There are many naysayers when it comes to having background noise while doing creative work. Well, THE KEY HERE IS THAT DIFFERENT PEOPLE FUNCTION DIFFERENTLY, so what works for me may not work for you. I highly encourage you to find an "attention buffer" that works for you, though!

3.   Exercise to get a boost of productivity

Okay, this is definitely my favorite trick, because it not only helps me increase my productivity, but it also keeps me healthy and sane. In addition to running, I take a few group classes at the nearest YMCA every week. When people try to make a point that I'm exercising "too much," I tell them I need some endorphins to manage stress.

Anyway, getting up, breathing in some fresh air, stretching and sweating a little bit is a welcome change when your work has you chained to a desk for hours on end. Gardening, walking the dog, chasing your kids around the park, going for a bike ride, dancing, and lifting weights... You can even prancercise[15] if you want to, just get moving already! These are all great ideas to fill in your breaks with some physical activity to compensate for all that mental hard work.

---

[15] http://en.wikipedia.org/wiki/Prancercise

When you exercise, you'll get the obvious health-related benefits, but you'll also be giving your brain a much-deserved break and possibly allowing it to solve any issues you may have encountered. In my case, it's usually a sentence that is difficult to crack, or a word that I can't quite translate naturally. People say they have their best ideas in the shower or when they're about to fall asleep; with me, it usually happens when I'm in the middle of a workout session and my brain can find an answer while working more passively.

Oftentimes you use all your energy to get the job done, ten you get completely drained, bored, stressed, and frustrated. So, instead of procrastinating, a better way to get things done without driving yourself mad is to get moving and push those problems to the background, so the answer can come to you more organically and without so many struggles.

In conclusion, you don't need to become a marathon runner or a triathlete to start enjoying the benefits of getting your blood flowing and your heart pumping. THE KEY HERE IS TO FIND AN ACTIVITY YOU TRULY ENJOY—otherwise, it's just more added stress!

Originally posted at
http://bit.ly/T3-Stress-and-Boredom

RECOMMENDED READING

Is it Possible to Balance Your Biggest Life Project —Your Children— and Working as a Translator?

By Rafa Lombardino

"Woman, what are you doing in front of the computer already?" or "How come you didn't answer the email I sent you half an hour ago?"

These were the two completely opposite reactions some of my clients had when I got back to work a few days after my children were born. The original plan was to take at least 45 days off for my maternity leave, then ease back into working part time to learn how to balance being a mother and a translator. I was back before the first 30 days were up...

Marissa was born September 2008 and Lorenzo was born August 2012. Both were born naturally in a birth tub at a small clinic, under the supervision of a midwife. In both occasions, I was released from the clinic a few hours later, and was back home to start my recovery, enjoy all the love from friends and family, and fall in love with my babies.

But it was not all a bed of roses. Raising a little one inside you demands a lot of energy during 40 weeks (or more!) Despite the immediate relief when your baby is finally in your arms, your body still needs time to go back to normal. You have to learn how to walk and sit down again after nine months doing things differently to accommodate the growing belly, the swollen feet, and the achy lower back.

What about your mind? Ah, your cheating mind... You end up switching day and night, depending on the routine imposed by your baby. Your thoughts may be clear in your head, but exhaustion and lack of sleep will end up interfering with your reasoning. You can bet it will!

Am I Going Crazy? — You open your mouth to say something you can't finish a sentence, trying to save up some energy and hoping everybody around you can read your mind.

You get frustrated when you drop everything, except for the baby and the precious milk you're pumping. By the way, if you want to enjoy the convenience of having bottles ready to go in the fridge, you'll spend at least three hours using a pump in four to five daily sessions. And here's a tip: fenugreek tea really works if your goal is to become a milking cow and produce 42 ounces of milk a day...

You actually start hearing voices! In my case, I couldn't fall asleep one night because the neighbors next door had a karaoke party going on and wouldn't stop singing Pat Benatar's "Hit Me With Your Best Shot" over and over again. The thing is that, when I opened the slide-glass door to the backyard, I realized it was all in my head. Maybe a mother's brain works in a different frequency when she has a newborn at home, so much so that it starts to pick up mysterious sound waves...

Despite all these unforeseen circumstances and what people may believe, taking care of a baby is not as complicated as it sounds. Actually, the complicated part is running after a four-year-old girl full of energy, who is going to half-day preschool Mondays, Wednesdays, and Fridays, does gymnastics on Tuesdays and Thursdays, dance on Fridays and still finds energy to outlast the Duracell bunny.

Four-year-olds can talk and their answer to everything is, "No!" They also work on a schedule: eating, bathing, doing homework, and going to bed. However, four-year-olds are capable of helping out, can go get the burp cloth, and give you a tight hug that recharges your own batteries.

Yes, babies depend on you for everything, but you soon get used to the cycle: feeding, changing diapers, putting down for a nap. And, if you're recovering without any surprises along the way, you can start planning to go back to work during the quieter times.

Making the Most of The Day — I'm the kind of person that can't sit still for too long. I need to always be doing something productive, so a few days after giving birth I already missed the sound of my keyboard as I type. However, taking into account all that physical, psychological, and emotional ups and downs, mothers need to be honest with themselves and ask the dreaded question: "Am I really ready?"

The last thing you want to do now is go back to work and turn your world upside down, making unforgivable mistakes, missing deadlines, and then blaming it all on sleepless nights. You need to know yourself well, learn when you're more productive, and plan everything accordingly.

Are you one of those who wakes up when it's still dark outside and can translate a thousand words before your stomach starts growling and demanding some breakfast? Great! If you went to bed at midnight, after walking around the house and singing all the lullabies you could remember until your baby finally fell asleep, just to wake up at three in the morning for another feeding, try to make the most of your insomnia and work for a couple of hours after your baby goes back to sleep. This way, you will get an early start and adapt yourself to your baby's routine.

Are you a night owl? Wonderful! Try to nap for at least one hour every time your baby falls asleep after a nice feeding and diaper change. The night will then be all yours to type your keyboard senseless.

When you find yourself stuck on an annoying expression, and the dictionary becomes useless when you try to render it naturally, take 15 minutes off to put a blanked on the floor and lay your baby on its belly, so he can work out its little arms and legs and learn how to support its head while training for some crawling. While you have fun watching your baby develop its motor skills, your mommy's mind will do some passive thinking. Several studies have found that your brain works better at finding a solution when you stop thinking about the problem and preoccupy yourself with another task, such as taking a shower, doing the dishes, doing the laundry, etc.

Use the minutes you spend breastfeeding or pumping to read the documents you're getting ready to translate, thus working on a preliminary sight translation while you skim through the original and "interpret" your translation out loud.

By the way, considering your hands will be busy very often, it could be a good idea to acquire some voice recognition software and dictate your translations to the computer. I have to confess that this option doesn't really work for me, because my brain works better with my fingers, rather than my mouth, so I'd rather to dictating. But, go ahead and see if it suits you.

No matter which technique works better for you, whenever you find a window to get back to work, focus on it and make the most of your productive minutes without feeling guilty before you get back to your mommy duties.

Your Baby and Your "Other Children" — Just like no two babies are exactly the same, translators are unique and have their own peculiarities. A couple of these tips may work for you, while you'll find others on your own. Still, remember that you're only one person and, the moment you become a mother, that's your main occupation.

Yes, it's hard to meet all of your baby's needs, as well as all the requirements made by your "other children." Nevertheless, good clients will understand you—they most likely went through the same thing—and, if they really like your work and appreciate your business relationship, they won't walk away.

Sometimes even the strictest clients will let their hearts melt when you send out a notice, months in advance, that you'll be taking maternity leave. I bet they—both men and women—

will ask you a thousand questions about how you're feeling, if you've already chosen the baby's name, and when you'll be due. Then they make you promise to send them some pictures as soon as the baby is born.

However, you'll find out that other clients really lack some empathy... In those cases, the best thing you can do is be realistic and bring your client back to Earth, insisting that you absolutely cannot translate 5,000 words worth of an extremely technical project by the end of the business day.

If your client still can't take "no" for an answer after you reminded him that you're on maternity leave, explained that you've given birth only three days ago, and are in no condition to go back to working regular business hours at the moment, the best thing you can do is to get graphic.

Tell your client you need to keep your feet elevated, because they're still a little puffy. It didn't work? Move on to the next level: explain that you can't sit for hours on end, because your lower belly still hurts from the pressure that your uterus is making on your nether regions, since the swell hasn't come down yet after spending nine-month in free expansion.

That still wasn't graphic enough? Ask your client—especially if you're talking to a *female* client—whether she knew that, after giving birth, women may bleed for six weeks and you still feel uncomfortable sitting down to work, even so during the first week, when you need to wear an adult diaper...

In most cases, when you're really driven to this kind of extreme, such a graphic image will help put your clients in perspective. They'll stop and think, "Wow! My translator has just had a baby and, here I am, asking her to do something that is already practically impossible under normal conditions!"

One of the following two things will most likely happen: you'll either find out that the project isn't really that urgent and can then negotiate a more realistic deadline, or your client will ask you whether you know someone you trust who could take on the project.

Secret Weapon — When you're ready to transition from maternity leave to part-time work, whether it is three days or three months after giving birth, it's always good to have a "secret weapon" to help you focus on your job.

In my case, the card I have up my sleeve is my husband, an A+ daddy who changes diapers, heats up a bottle, puts the baby on a rocking chair or on its tummy to get a work out. Your secret weapon could be your parents, in-laws, siblings, friends...

Finding support is crucial and everybody wins: you can go back to organizing your schedule and your company enjoys some one-on-one time with the baby. The little one will also benefit from this arrangement, since interacting with different people will help its developing brain to study different facial expressions, identify other voices, and memorize characteristics of people who will play an important role in its little life.

Believe me: juggling the thousands of things you need to do throughout the day is possible. Plan ahead and rely on your organization skills, making notes on your good-old paper planner or your Google calendar. The secret is not biting off more than you can chew and being honest with yourself.

Thinking about all these pros and cons, all these ups and downs, if I had a chance to do it all over again I actually wouldn't change a single comma in my story.

**Originally posted in Portuguese
on Lorena Leandro's blog
Ao principiante
http://bit.ly/T3-children**

EXTRAS

Business Draft Plan
*Fill out the form below to create
a draft for your business plan*

Short-Term Goals (1-5 Years)

1. _____

2. _____

3. _____

4. _____

5. _____

Long-Term Goals (10+ Years)

1. _____

2. _____

3. _____

4. _____

5. _____

Desired Business Names

Do a Google search to check if your desired name has already been taken. Beware of names that have been registered by other businesses or sound too similar.

1. _____

2. _____

3. _____

Desired Business Logo

Enter a description of the logo you visualized or, if you're a great artist, draw a picture into the space provided below. Once you sit down at the computer to work on it, beware of pictures copied from the Internet, because they are most likely copyright protected.

Slogan

Try to be as catchy as possible, so clients can identify the slogan with your business.

Mission Statement

Enter a few words about the purpose of your business.

Target Audience

Enter a few words about the purpose of your business.

Other Business Plan Components
Use this space to describe other materials you would add to your strategy.

_____

_____

_____

_____

_____

_____

_____

_____

_____

_____

EXTRAS

Glossary: Key Terms for Translators

- **100% Matches** — When working with Computer-Assisted Translation tools, the program will be able to identify sentences that are identical to something translated in the past and recorded to a Translation Memory. These instances can be populated automatically, based on that past translation, but should still be proofread for consistency, in the likely event that the context in which it's being used is somewhat different.

- **1099** — A form created by the U.S. Internal Revenue Services (IRS) and filed by a company during tax season to report payments made to a service provider. One copy of the 1099 is submitted to the Tax Department and the other is sent to the Service Provider (a translator or interpreter, in this context.) It contains information on how much the company paid out in miscellaneous income to an individual who is not a company employee.

- **Back Translation** — Depending on the client's preferences, it will be a rough draft (word for word) or a final draft (readable version) of a translation back into the original source language (Language A → Language B → Language A).

- **Certificate of Translation** — A letter in which translators identify themselves, list their credentials and mention a project they have completed, while stating that their translation is a true and faithful version of the original. At the bottom of this short letter, you can add the legal template required of your state, so that a notary can fill in the information (his/her name and date) to sign, stamp, and notarize your statement.

- **Clean File** — A monolingual document, available in ONE language only, usually the target language after the translation process is thoroughly completed. Some clients request that only a clean file be delivered, especially those who don't work with Computer-Assisted Translation tools.

- **Cloud Storage** — Online service that allows users to store files on their servers in a remote location, so that they can be retrieved by logging into a website from any computer, as long there is an internet connection available.

- **Computer-Assisted Translation (CAT)** — Software used by translators to record their translations into a database. Therefore, human intervention is required. CAT Tools break down files of different formats, isolating Segments for translation, so that Translation Units can be added to a Translation Memory. Examples include Trados, Wordfast, memoQ, OmegaT, DejaVu, and Swordfish, among others.

- **Crowdsourcing** — When companies turn to people who aren't in their payroll to try and solve an issue, instead of using their own human resources or hiring advisors. In the T&I industry, it takes place when a company "hires a crowd" to translate their website, publication, or other material. This request is often made without any promise of compensation, or maybe in exchange for some incentives and perks, such as a free premium account on the website of the company that the crowd is called upon to help, or a "web badge" that members of the crowdsourcing project can display on their personal website.

- **Desktop Publishing (DTP)** — The act of planning the layout and overall look of a document. DTP elements may include bold, italics, underline, font color and size, which are also common features found in word processors, but also tables, graphics, and images that demand the use of publication software, which are programs applied by advertising and publishing companies to design flyers, brochures, reports, newspapers, magazines, books, and any other type of professional-looking publications.

- **Editing** — Checking a document for typos, misspelled words, grammar errors, and overall style. May be also called "Copyediting," "Proofreading," or "Reviewing," depending on the client's preferences, so it's safer to always check exactly what services they are requesting.

- **File Transfer Protocol (FTP)** — A method used to transfer files between two computers, mostly used in the T&I industry for translators to download a large project from a client's FTP site, then submit their translation back without using emails.

- **Fuzzy Matches** — When working with Computer-Assisted Translation tools, the program will be able to identify new sentences that are 50%-99% similar to something you've translated in the past and recorded to a Translation Memory. These are called "fuzzy matches."

- **Hybrid Translation** — Some Computer-Assisted Translation tools nowadays work with both Machine Translations (material pulled from Google Translate, for example) and Human Translations (which you type yourself and save to your Translation Memory, in addition to the glossaries you've been compiling within these programs to ensure vocabulary consistency). However, you only activate machine translation suggestions if you want to, because the software will not do so by itself (human intervention is always needed).

- **HTML — HyperText Markup Language** used to write webpages for the Internet. One of the formats compatible with CAT tools to facilitate the localization of websites.

- **Invoice —** A bill that a service provider sends a client to request payment for services rendered.

- **Localization —** Adjusting a language project for a certain location by adapting software or hardware for non-native environments and other countries and cultures.

- **Machine Translation (MT) —** No human intervention required; software-based translations. Most programs work on word-for-word replacement. Others learn to improve automatic translations according to user's suggestions.

- **Non-Compete Agreement (NCA) —** An agreement signed between a service provider and the company they are working with, in which the service provider agrees not to establish direct contact with end clients, unless upon request by the company itself.

- **Non-Disclosure Agreement (NDA) —** An agreement signed between a service provider and the company they are working with, in which the service provider agrees not to disclose any confidential information about their client.

- **Output —** Your production in either Words Per Hour (WPH) or Words per Day (WPD), according to the average number of words you can translate in that given amount of time. Do not mistake it for Words Per Minute (WPM), which is a unit of measure related to typing speed, not translation.

- **PHP —** Hypertext Preprocessor, a cross-platform server-side scripting language used to create dynamic web pages.

One of the formats compatible with Computer-Assisted Translation tools to facilitate web localization projects.

- **Post-Editing Machine Translation (PEMT)** — Editing a document that has been translated by a Machine Translation program, whether you have access to the source document or not.

- **Project Manager (PM)** — Someone working for a translation agency or language department inside a large corporation, who is in charge of assigning translation projects to translators.

- **Proofreading** — Checking a document for typos, misspelled words, grammar errors, and overall style. May be also called "Copyediting," "Editing," or "Reviewing," depending on the client's preferences, so it's safer to always check exactly what services they are requesting.

- **Purchase Order (PO)** — A document confirming that a project was assigned to an independent service provider. It usually states project description, assignment and delivery dates, and a reference number to be used by contractors on their invoice.

- **Quality Assurance (QA)** — The last step of a translation project, when the last details of a document are checked to ensure overall quality. There are ISO and ASTM standards that address the subject, but this step can be performed by a professional reviewer or a specialized software to check inconsistencies (when the same term was translated differently throughout the text,) terms that deviate from a project glossary, omissions, target segments that are identical to source segments, punctuation mistakes, capitalization and number value/formatting errors, and incorrect untranslatables and tags.

- **Quote** — While negotiating a project, translators will send their clients a quote that includes the total price for the project and what the proposed delivery deadline would be. Once a quote is approved, a client will send a confirmation, most likely in the form of a Purchase Order.

- **Repetitions** — When working with Computer-Assisted Translation tools, the program will be able to identify identical sentences within the current file or set of files being translated. Once the sentence is translated the first time it appears and, consequently recorded to the Translation Memory, all subsequent instances can be populated automatically based on that translation.

- **Reviewing** — Checking a document for typos, misspelled words, grammar errors, and overall style. May be also called "Copyediting," "Editing," or "Proofreading," depending on the client's preferences, so it's safer to always check exactly what services they are requesting.

- **Segments** — Each unit of text isolated by a Computer-Assisted Translation tools for translation. It can be a sentence or a title—anything that the program interprets as a separate unit of text.

- **Sight Translation** — The act of reading a source document in the target language. For example, the translator receives a document in Language A and reads it aloud in Language B so those present can understand the content.

- **Termbase (TB)** — A terminology database that functions as a glossary, to which translators enter their preferred terms while using a Computer-Assisted Translation tools. After a term is entered into a TB and it later appears on a segment, the program identifies it and shows the respective translation as a suggestion.

- **Track Changes** — A setting in word processors that records all changes made to a document, leaving revision marks as a proofreading history. Changes can then be accepted or rejected before the final version of the document is saved.

- **Translation Environment Tool (TEnT)** — See "Computer-Assisted Translation (CAT)."

- **Translation Memory (TM)** — Database created by Computer-Assisted Translation tools during the translation process in order to record Translation Units and thus identify fuzzy matches and repetitions.

- **Translation Unit (TU)** — The combination of a source sentence and a target sentence that is recorded into a Translation Memory.

- **Unclean File** — A bilingual document, available in two languages (one "layer" on top of the other) after the translation process is carried out, but before the file is completed ("cleaned"). Some clients request that an "unclean file" be delivered, so that they can forward it to Quality Assurance or Proofreading team for the applicable changes to be made and the updated bilingual material to be later uploaded to their own Translation Memory.

- **W9** — A form created by the U.S. Internal Revenue Services (IRS) called "Request for Taxpayer Identification Number and Certification," which is filed by U.S. persons—both citizens and residents paying income tax in the United States—to provide relevant information to companies with which they do business with in the capacity of a service provider or vendor, not an employee.

- **Work Order — See** "Purchase Order (PO)."

EXTRAS

Software Ideas

○ **Accounting and Invoicing**
- ✓ **Crunch**
  http://bit.ly/T3-Crunch
- ✓ **Express Accounts**
  http://bit.ly/T3-ExAccounts
- ✓ **Express Invoice**
  http://bit.ly/T3-ExInvoice
- ✓ **GNU Cash**
  http://bit.ly/T3-GNUCash
- ✓ **Invoice365**
  http://bit.ly/T3-Invoice365
- ✓ **MoneyLine**
  http://bit.ly/T3-MoneyLine
- ✓ **Mint**
  http://bit.ly/T3-Mint
- ✓ **Outright**
  http://bit.ly/T3-Outright
- ✓ **TurboTax**
  http://bit.ly/T3-TurboTax
- ✓ **QuickBooks**
  http://bit.ly/T3-QuickBooks
- ✓ **Quicken**
  http://bit.ly/T3-Quicken

○ **Audio Editing**
- ✓ **Audacity**
  http://bit.ly/T3-Audacity
- ✓ **DJ Audio Editor**
  http://bit.ly/T3-DJAudio

- ○ **Backup Solutions**
  - ✓ **Backup Runner**
    http://bit.ly/T3-BackupRunner
  - ✓ **Carbonite**
    http://bit.ly/T3-Carbonite
  - ✓ **Dropbox**
    http://bit.ly/T3-Dropbox
  - ✓ **My Backup Drive**
    http://bit.ly/T3-MyBuDrive

- ○ **Business Management**
  - ✓ **Business PlanMaker**
    http://bit.ly/T3-BizPlanMaker

- ○ **CAT Tools**
  - ✓ **Abbyy SmartCAT**
    http://bit.ly/T3-AbbyCAT
  - ✓ **Across**
    http://bit.ly/T3-Across
  - ✓ **Anaphraseus**
    http://bit.ly/T3-Anaphraseus
  - ✓ **AnyMem**
    http://bit.ly/T3-AnyMem
  - ✓ **CAT Count**
    http://bit.ly/T3-CATCount
  - ✓ **DéjàVu**
    http://bit.ly/T3-Dejavu
  - ✓ **Google Translator Toolkit**
    http://bit.ly/T3-GoogleToolkit
  - ✓ **Jive Fusion**
    http://bit.ly/T3-JiveFusion
  - ✓ **memoQ**
    http://bit.ly/T3-memoQ
  - ✓ **MetaTexis**
    http://bit.ly/T3-MetaTexis

- ✓ OmegaT
  http://bit.ly/T3-OmegaT
- ✓ **Open Language Tools**
  http://bit.ly/T3-OpenLangTools
- ✓ **Passolo**
  http://bit.ly/T3-Passolo
- ✓ **SDL-Trados**
  http://bit.ly/T3-Trados
- ✓ **Star Transit**
  http://bit.ly/T3-StarTransit
- ✓ **Stingray Alignment Editor**
  http://bit.ly/T3-Stingray
- ✓ **Swordfish Translation Editor**
  http://bit.ly/T3-Swordfish
- ✓ **Wordfast**
  http://bit.ly/T3-Wordfast

- o Dictation & Transcription
  - ✓ **Dragon Speech Recognition**
    http://bit.ly/T3-NuanceDragon
  - ✓ **E-speaking**
    http://bit.ly/T3-eSpeaking
  - ✓ **Express Dictate**
    http://bit.ly/T3-ExDictate
  - ✓ **Express Scribe**
    http://bit.ly/T3-ExScribe
  - ✓ **InqScribe**
    http://bit.ly/T3-InqScribe
  - ✓ **TextShark**
    http://bit.ly/T3-TextShark
  - ✓ **Transana**
    http://bit.ly/T3-Transana
  - ✓ **Transcribe**
    http://bit.ly/T3-Transcribe
  - ✓ **VoiceScript**
    http://bit.ly/T3-VoiceScript

- File Converters
  - ✓ Able2Doc
    http://bit.ly/T3-Able2Doc
  - ✓ Able2Extract
    http://bit.ly/T3-Able2Ext
  - ✓ Adobe Acrobat
    http://bit.ly/T30AdobePDF
  - ✓ Adobe Acrobat Reader
    http://bit.ly/T3-AcrobatReader
  - ✓ Adobe PDF Online Conversion Tools
    http://bit.ly/T3-AdobeOnline
  - ✓ Convert PDF to Word
    http://bit.ly/T3-ConvertPDF-Word
  - ✓ CutePDF
    http://bit.ly/T3-CutePDF
  - ✓ DeskPDF Creator
    http://bit.ly/T3-DeskPDFCreator
  - ✓ DeskPDF Editor
    http://bit.ly/T3-DeskPDFEditor
  - ✓ Desk-UN-PDF Converter
    http://bit.ly/T3-DeskPDFConverter
  - ✓ DOC To PDF
    http://bit.ly/T3-Doc-PDF
  - ✓ DoPDF
    http://bit.ly/T3-DoPDF
  - ✓ Doxillion Document Converter Software
    http://bit.ly/T3-Doxillion
  - ✓ Excel-to-PDF Converter
    http://bit.ly/T3-ExcelPDF
  - ✓ FoxIt Phantom
    http://bit.ly/T3-FoxitPhantom
  - ✓ Foxit Reader
    http://bit.ly/T3-FoxitReader
  - ✓ Neevia
    http://bit.ly/T3-Neevia

- ✓ **NitroPDF**
  http://bit.ly/T3-Nitro
- ✓ **Nuance PDF Converter**
  http://bit.ly/T3-NuancePDFConv
- ✓ **PDF Converter**
  http://bit.ly/T3-FreePDF
- ✓ **PDF on Fly**
  http://bit.ly/T3-PDFFly
- ✓ **PDF Online**
  http://bit.ly/T3-PDFOnline
- ✓ **PDF-to-Text Converter**
  http://bit.ly/T3-PDFText
- ✓ **PPT-to-PDF Converter**
  http://bit.ly/T3-PPTPDF
- ✓ **PrimoPDF**
  http://bit.ly/T3-Primo
- ✓ **Smart PDF Creator**
  http://bit.ly/T3-SmartPDF
- ✓ **Word-to-PDF Converter**
  http://bit.ly/T3-WordPDF
- ✓ **ZamZar**
  http://bit.ly/T3-Zamzar

- ○ File Creators
  - ✓ **OpenOffice**
    http://bit.ly/T3-OpenOffice
  - ✓ **LibreOffice**
    http://bit.ly/T3-LibreOffice

- ○ Glossaries
  - ✓ **AcroLexic**
    http://bit.ly/T3-AcroLexic
  - ✓ **AnyLexic**
    http://bit.ly/T3-AnyLexic
  - ✓ **Babylon**
    http://bit.ly/T3-Babylon

- ✓ **Dictionary Organizer Deluxe**
  http://bit.ly/T3-DicDeluxe
- ✓ **GlossWord**
  http://bit.ly/T3-GlossWord
- ✓ **WinLexic**
  http://bit.ly/T3-WinLexic

- o Image Editing
  - ✓ **GNU Image Manipulation Program (GIMP)**
    http://bit.ly/T3-GIMP
  - ✓ **PhotoStudio Expressions**
    http://bit.ly/T3-PhotoStudio

- o Optical Character Recognition (OCRs)
  - ✓ **ABBYY FineReader**
    http://bit.ly/T3-Invoice365
  - ✓ **Free OCR**
    http://bit.ly/T3-FreeOCR
  - ✓ **MegaOCR**
    http://bit.ly/T3-MegaOCR
  - ✓ **New OCR**
    http://bit.ly/T3-NewOCR
  - ✓ **OmniPage**
    http://bit.ly/T3-NuanceOmnipage
  - ✓ **Prime OCR**
    http://bit.ly/T3-PrimeOCR
  - ✓ **Simple OCR**
    http://bit.ly/T3-SimpleOCR

- o Project Management
  - ✓ **AnyTime Organizer**
    http://bit.ly/T3-AnyTime
  - ✓ **Express Project Management**
    http://bit.ly/T3-ExPM
  - ✓ **Projectex**
    http://bit.ly/T3-Projetex

- ✓ **Translation Office 3000**
  http://bit.ly/T3-TO3000
- ✓ **VIP Organizer**
  http://bit.ly/T3-VIPOrg
- ✓ **VIP Task Manager Standard Edition**
  http://bit.ly/T3-VIPTask

- ○ **Slide Presentations**
  - ✓ **Express Points**
    http://bit.ly/T3-ExPoints
  - ✓ **Prezi**
    http://bit.ly/T3-Prezi

- ○ **Subtitling**
  - ✓ **Video Watermark Subtitle Creator**
    http://bit.ly/T3-Watermark
  - ✓ **Xilisoft**
    http://bit.ly/T3-Xilisoft

- ○ **Translation Memory (TM) & Terminology Base (TB)**
  - ✓ **Anymem**
    http://bit.ly/T3-AnyMemTM
  - ✓ **Felix TM Management**
    http://bit.ly/T3-FelixTM
  - ✓ **MyMemory**
    http://bit.ly/T3-MyMemory
  - ✓ **Olifant TM Editor**
    http://bit.ly/T3-Olifant
  - ✓ **TinyTM**
    http://bit.ly/T3-TinyTM
  - ✓ **TuMatXa Repository**
    http://bit.ly/T3-TuMatXa
  - ✓ **Very Large Translation Memory Project**
    http://bit.ly/T3-VLTM
  - ✓ **Xbench**
    http://bit.ly/T3-XBench

- o Typing
  - ✓ **FastFox Text Expander**
    http://bit.ly/T3-FastFox
  - ✓ **KeyBlaze Typing Tutor**
    http://bit.ly/T3-KeyBlaze
  - ✓ **Typing Instructor**
    http://bit.ly/T3-TypingInstructor
  - ✓ **Typing Quick & Easy**
    http://bit.ly/T3-TypingQuickEasy

- o Word Count
  - ✓ **AnyCount**
    http://bit.ly/T3-AnyCount
  - ✓ **ClipCount**
    http://bit.ly/T3-ClipCount
  - ✓ **Word Count 'N' Invoice**
    http://bit.ly/T3-WordCountInvoice

- o ZIP Compression
  - ✓ **Express Zip**
    http://bit.ly/T3-ExZip
  - ✓ **Sanmaxi Zip Repair**
    http://bit.ly/T3-Sanmaxi
  - ✓ **Universal Extractor**
    http://bit.ly/T3-UniExt
  - ✓ **WinZip**
    http://bit.ly/T3-WinZip

EXTRAS

Useful Links

o **Books**

✓ **"Is That a Fish in Your Ear"**
By David Bellos
http://bit.ly/T3-FishEar

✓ **"Found in Translation"**
By Nataly Kelly and Jost Zetzsche
http://bit.ly/T3-FoundTranslation

✓ **"The Entrepreneurial Linguist"**
By Judy & Dagmar Jenner
http://bit.ly/T3-Entrepreneurs

✓ **"How to Succeed as a Freelance Translator"**
By Corinne McKay
http://bit.ly/T3-SucceedFreelancer

✓ **"Thoughts on Translation"**
By Corinne McKay
http://bit.ly/T3-ThoughtsTranslation

✓ **"The Prosperous Translator"**
By Chris Durban
http://bit.ly/T3-ProsperousTranslator

✓ **"The Three Percent Problem"**
By Chad W. Post
http://bit.ly/T3-ThreePercent

- ✓ **"In Translation"**
  By Esther Allen and Susan Bernofsky
  http://bit.ly/T3-InTranslation

- ✓ **"Why Translation Matters"**
  By Edith Grossman
  http://bit.ly/T3-WhyTranslation

- ✓ **"The Man Between"**
  By Michael Henry Heim
  http://bit.ly/T3-ManBetween

- ✓ **"Diversification in the Language Industry"**
  By Nicole Y Adams
  http://bit.ly/T3-Diversification

- ✓ **"101 Things a Translator Needs to Know"**
  By WLF Think Tank
  http://bit.ly/T3-101Things

- ✓ **"Through The Language Glass"**
  By Guy Deutscher
  http://bit.ly/T3-LanguageGlass

- ✓ **"Translation and Globalization"**
  By Michael Cronin
  http://bit.ly/T3-Globalization

- ✓ **"Translation in the Digital Age"**
  By Michael Cronin
  http://bit.ly/T3-DigitalAge

MORE BOOKS ON TRANSLATION
http://bit.ly/T3-TranslationBooks

- Bookmarking
  - ✓ **Bitly**
    http://bit.ly/T3-BitLy
  - ✓ **Delicious**
    http://bit.ly/T3-Delicious
  - ✓ **Diigo**
    http://bit.ly/T3-Diigo
  - ✓ **Google Bookmarks**
    http://bit.ly/T3-GoogleBookmarks
  - ✓ **HubPages**
    http://bit.ly/T3-HubPages
  - ✓ **Licorize.com**
    http://bit.ly/T3-Licorize
  - ✓ **Reddit on Translations**
    http://bit.ly/T3-Reddit
  - ✓ **Stumble Upon**
    http://bit.ly/T3-StumbleUpon

- Business Assistance
  - ✓ **Counselors for America's Small Business**
    http://bit.ly/T3-Score
  - ✓ **U.S. Small Business Administration**
    http://bit.ly/T3-SBA

- Business Entities
  - ✓ **C Corporation**
    http://bit.ly/T3-CCorp
  - ✓ **Corporation**
    http://bit.ly/T3-Corp
  - ✓ **Limited Liability Company**
    http://bit.ly/T3-LLC
  - ✓ **Limited Liability Limited Partnership**
    http://bit.ly/T3-LLCPartner
  - ✓ **Partnership**
    http://bit.ly/T3-Partner

- ✓ S Corporation
  http://bit.ly/T3-SCorp
- ✓ Sole Proprietorship
  http://bit.ly/T3-SoleProp

○ Calendar and Workflow Websites
  - ✓ Bravenet
    http://bit.ly/T3-Bravenet
  - ✓ Calendarix
    http://bit.ly/T3-Calendarix
  - ✓ ConnectDaily
    http://bit.ly/T3-ConnectDaily
  - ✓ ContactOffice
    http://bit.ly/T3-ContactOffice
  - ✓ Google Calendar
    http://bit.ly/T3-GoogleCalendar
  - ✓ KeepAndShare
    http://bit.ly/T3-KeepShare
  - ✓ LoCalendar
    http://bit.ly/T3-LoCalendar
  - ✓ Trello
    http://bit.ly/T3-Trello
  - ✓ WebOffice.com
    http://bit.ly/T3-WebOffice

○ Client Education Resources Provided by the ATA
  - ✓ ATA's Business Smarts Column
    http://bit.ly/T3-BizSmarts
  - ✓ ATA's Getting It Right for Translators
    http://bit.ly/T3-RightTrans
  - ✓ ATA's Getting It Right for Interpreters
    http://bit.ly/T3-RightInterp
  - ✓ ATA's Standards For Buying A Non-Commodity
    http://bit.ly/T3-NonCommodity

- ○ Crowdfunding
  - ✓ **Angels Den**
    http://bit.ly/T3-AngelsDen
  - ✓ **Angel List**
    http://bit.ly/T3-AngelList
  - ✓ **Bolstr**
    http://bit.ly/T3-Bolstr
  - ✓ **Circle Up**
    http://bit.ly/T3-CircleUp
  - ✓ **Fundable**
    http://bit.ly/T3-Fundable
  - ✓ **FundAnything**
    http://bit.ly/T3-FundAnything
  - ✓ **FundedByMe**
    http://bit.ly/T3-FundedByMe
  - ✓ **Go Fund Me**
    http://bit.ly/T3-GoFundMe
  - ✓ **Invested In**
    http://bit.ly/T3-InvestedIn
  - ✓ **IndieGogo**
    http://bit.ly/T3-IndieGogo
  - ✓ **KickStarter**
    http://bit.ly/T3-KickStarter
  - ✓ **Pozible**
    http://bit.ly/T3-Pozible
  - ✓ **PubSlush**
    http://bit.ly/T3-PubSlush
  - ✓ **Seedrs**
    http://bit.ly/T3-Seedrs
  - ✓ **Sponsume**
    http://bit.ly/T3-Sponsume
  - ✓ **Symbid**
    http://bit.ly/T3-Symbid
  - ✓ **Tilt**
    http://bit.ly/T3-Tilt

- ✓ Unbound
  http://bit.ly/T3-Unbound
- ✓ We Funder
  http://bit.ly/T3-WeFunder

○ Discussion Forums
  - ✓ English Spanish Translator
    http://bit.ly/T3-ENESForum
  - ✓ Proz.com Forum
    http://bit.ly/T3-ProzForum
  - ✓ Translation Directory Forum
    http://bit.ly/T3-TransDirForum
  - ✓ TranslatorsBase Forum
    http://bit.ly/T3-TransBaseForum
  - ✓ Translators Cafe Forum
    http://bit.ly/T3-TranslatorsCafeForum
  - ✓ WordReference Forum
    http://bit.ly/T3-WordReferenceForum

○ Freelancing
  - ✓ Crunch on Freelancing
    http://bit.ly/T3-CrunchFree
  - ✓ Freelance Folder
    http://bit.ly/T3-FreeFolder
  - ✓ Life Hacker on Freelancing
    http://bit.ly/T3-LifeHacker
  - ✓ Reddit on Freelancing
    http://bit.ly/T3-RedditFree

Google Docs Resources
  - ✓ Google Drive Training
    http://bit.ly/T3-GDTraining
  - ✓ Google Groups
    http://bit.ly/T3-GDGroups

- ✓ **Google Docs Forum**
  http://bit.ly/T3-GDForum
- ✓ **Google Docs Guide: How to do Stuff with Google Docs**
  http://bit.ly/T3-GDGuide
- ✓ **Google Docs in Plain English (Video)**
  http://bit.ly/T3-GDVideo
- ✓ **Google Docs Offline Access**
  http://bit.ly/T3-GDOffline
- ✓ **Official Google Drive Blog**
  http://bit.ly/T3-GDBlog

- ○ Images Databases
  - ✓ **Free Range Photos (Free Pictures)**
    http://bit.ly/T3-FreeRangePhotos
  - ✓ **Gratisography (Free Pictures)**
    http://bit.ly/T3-Gratisography
  - ✓ **Jay Mantri (Free Pictures)**
    http://bit.ly/T3-JayMantri
  - ✓ **Life of Pix (Free Pictures)**
    http://bit.ly/T3-LifeOfPix
  - ✓ **Little Visuals (Free Pictures)**
    http://bit.ly/T3-LittleVisuals
  - ✓ **Magdeleine (Free Pictures)**
    http://bit.ly/T3-Magdeleine
  - ✓ **New Old Stock (Free Pictures)**
    http://bit.ly/T3-NewOldStock
  - ✓ **Picography (Free Pictures)**
    http://bit.ly/T3-Pixabay
  - ✓ **Pic Jumbo (Free Pictures)**
    http://bit.ly/T3-PicJumbo
  - ✓ **Pixabay (Free Pictures)**
    http://bit.ly/T3-Pixabay
  - ✓ **Public Domain Archive (Free Pictures)**
    http://bit.ly/T3-PDArch
  - ✓ **Snapographic (Free Pictures)**
    http://bit.ly/T3-Snapographic

- ✓ **Split Shire (Free Pictures)**
  http://bit.ly/T3-SplitShire
- ✓ **Unrestricted Stock (Free Pictures)**
  http://bit.ly/T3-UnrestStock
- ✓ **Unsplash (Free Pictures)**
  http://bit.ly/T3-Unsplash

- o Invoicing (Online Solutions)
  - ✓ **Billing Orchard**
    http://bit.ly/T3-Orchard
  - ✓ **Blinksale**
    http://bit.ly/T3-Blinksale
  - ✓ **Cashboard**
    http://bit.ly/T3-Cashboard
  - ✓ **FreshBooks**
    http://bit.ly/T3-FreshBooks
  - ✓ **Invoice Machine**
    http://bit.ly/T3-InvoiceMachine
  - ✓ **Invoice Place**
    http://bit.ly/T3-InvoicePlace
  - ✓ **Invotrak**
    http://bit.ly/T3-Invotrak
  - ✓ **Less Accounting**
    http://bit.ly/T3-LessAcc
  - ✓ **Side Job Track**
    http://bit.ly/T3-SideJobTrack
  - ✓ **Simple Invoices**
    http://bit.ly/T3-SimpleInvoices
  - ✓ **Simplybill**
    http://bit.ly/T3-Simplybill

- o Job Boards
  - ✓ **Aquarius**
    http://bit.ly/T3-Aquarius
  - ✓ **Elance**
    http://bit.ly/T3-Elance

- ✓ **Foreign Word**
  http://bit.ly/T3-ForeignWord
- ✓ **Freelancer.com**
  http://bit.ly/T3-Freelancer
- ✓ **iFreelance**
  http://bit.ly/T3-iFreelance
- ✓ **LangMates**
  http://bit.ly/T3-LangMates
- ✓ **Language123**
  http://bit.ly/T3-Language123
- ✓ **Linguist Finder**
  http://bit.ly/T3-LinguistFinder
- ✓ **Linguist List**
  http://bit.ly/T3-LinguistList
- ✓ **Proz**
  http://bit.ly/T3-Proz
- ✓ **TraduGuide**
  http://bit.ly/T3-TraduGuide
- ✓ **Translation Portal**
  http://bit.ly/T3-TranslationPortal
- ✓ **Translators Base**
  http://bit.ly/T3-TranslatorsBase
- ✓ **Translators Cafe**
  http://bit.ly/T3-TranslatorsCafe
- ✓ **Translator Pub**
  http://bit.ly/T3-TranslatorPub
- ✓ **Translators Town**
  http://bit.ly/T3-TranslatorsTown

- ○ Language Codes
  - ✓ **ISO 639-2**
    http://bit.ly/T3-ISO

- ○ Machine Translations (MTs)
  - ✓ **Bing**
    http://bit.ly/T3-MTBing

- ✓ Dictionary.com
  http://bit.ly/T3-MTDic
- ✓ **Google Translate**
  http://bit.ly/T3-MTGT
- ✓ **NeuroTran**
  http://bit.ly/T3-MTNeuroTran
- ✓ **Online Translator**
  http://bit.ly/T3-MTOT
- ✓ **PROMT**
  http://bit.ly/T3-ProMT
- ✓ **Reverso**
  http://bit.ly/T3-MTReverso
- ✓ **SDL FreeTranslation**
  http://bit.ly/T3-MTSDL
- ✓ **Smart Translator**
  http://bit.ly/T3-MTSmart
- ✓ **Systran**
  http://bit.ly/T3-MTSystran
- ✓ **WinBabel**
  http://bit.ly/T3-MTWinBabel
- ✓ **WordLingo**
  http://bit.ly/T3-MTWordLingo

- ○ **Marketing Materials**
  - ✓ **About Technology on Promotional Items**
    http://bit.ly/T3-AboutPromo
  - ✓ **Amsterdam Printing**
    http://bit.ly/T3-Amsterdam
  - ✓ **Branders**
    http://bit.ly/T3-Branders
  - ✓ **Leader Promos**
    http://bit.ly/T3-LeaderPromos
  - ✓ **Myron**
    http://bit.ly/T3-Myron
  - ✓ **Superior Promos**
    http://bit.ly/T3-SuperiorPromos

- ✓ Vista Print
  http://bit.ly/T3-VistaPrint

- ○ **Publications**
  - ✓ **1611**
    http://bit.ly/T3-1611
  - ✓ **Cultus Journal**
    http://bit.ly/T3-Cultus
  - ✓ **Doletiana**
    http://bit.ly/T3-Doletiana
  - ✓ **eWordNews**
    http://bit.ly/T3-eWordNews
  - ✓ **inTRAlinea**
    http://bit.ly/T3-inTRAlinea
  - ✓ **IATIS Bulletin**
    http://bit.ly/T3-IATIS
  - ✓ **ITIA Bulletin**
    http://bit.ly/T3-ITIA
  - ✓ **JoSTrans**
    http://bit.ly/T3-JoSTrans
  - ✓ **Metamorphoses**
    http://bit.ly/T3-Metamorphoses
  - ✓ **Saltana**
    http://bit.ly/T3-Saltana
  - ✓ **Translation: A Transdisciplinary Journal**
    http://bit.ly/T3-FUSP
  - ✓ **Translation & Interpreting**
    http://bit.ly/T3-TransInt
  - ✓ **Translation Journal**
    http://bit.ly/T3-TransJournal
  - ✓ **Translorial**
    http://bit.ly/T3-Translorial

- ○ **Rates & Payment**
  - ✓ **ATA's Translator Earnings Calculator**
    http://bit.ly/T3-ATACalc

- ✓ **Blacklist by Translation Ethics**
  http://bit.ly/T3-BlackList
- ✓ **Black Sheep (Translation Companies With Payment Issues) — a LinkedIn Group**
  http://bit.ly/T3-BlackSheep
- ✓ **Budgeting for Your Translation Projects**
  http://bit.ly/T3-Budgeting
- ✓ **Cost of Translation and Localization Services**
  http://bit.ly/T3-CostOfTrans
- ✓ **Detecting and Reacting to False Job Offers and other Scams**
  http://bit.ly/T3-TranslationScams
- ✓ **Future of Translation**
  http://bit.ly/T3-Future
- ✓ **Payment Practices**
  http://bit.ly/T3-PaymentPractices
- ✓ **PayPal**
  http://bit.ly/T3-PayPal
- ✓ **Skrill**
  http://bit.ly/T3-Skrill
- ✓ **Proz.com Rate Calculator**
  http://bit.ly/T3-ProzCalc
- ✓ **Translator Client Review List**
  http://bit.ly/T3-TCRList
- ✓ **Translation Ethics**
  http://bit.ly/T3-TranslationEthics
- ✓ **Translation Payments**
  http://bit.ly/T3-TranslationPayments

- ○ **Social Networking Websites**
  - ✓ **AboutMe**
    http://bit.ly/T3-AboutMe
  - ✓ **Academia**
    http://bit.ly/T3-Academia
  - ✓ **Busuu**
    http://bit.ly/T3-Busuu

- ✓ **1099**
  http://bit.ly/T3-1099
- ✓ **Facebook**
  http://bit.ly/T3-Facebook
- ✓ **Fiverr**
  http://bit.ly/T3-Fiverr
- ✓ **Goodreads**
  http://bit.ly/T3-GoodReads
- ✓ **Google+**
  http://bit.ly/T3-GooglePlus
- ✓ **Instagram**
  http://bit.ly/T3-Instagram
- ✓ **iTalki**
  http://bit.ly/T3-iTalki
- ✓ **Library Thing**
  http://bit.ly/T3-LibraryThing
- ✓ **LinkedIn**
  http://bit.ly/T3-LinkedIn
- ✓ **LiveMocha**
  http://bit.ly/T3-LiveMocha
- ✓ **MeetUp**
  http://bit.ly/T3-MeetUp
- ✓ **Pinterest**
  http://bit.ly/T3-Pinterest
- ✓ **Plaxo**
  http://bit.ly/T3-Plaxo
- ✓ **Sonico**
  http://bit.ly/T3-Sonico
- ✓ **TalkBizNow**
  http://bit.ly/T3-TalkBizNow
- ✓ **Twitter**
  http://bit.ly/T3-Twitter
- ✓ **Wattpad**
  http://bit.ly/T3-WattPad
- ✓ **WeHeartIt**
  http://bit.ly/T3-WeHeartIt

- ✓ **Zoopa**
  http://bit.ly/T3-Zoopa

- ○ Translation Service Agreement Templates
  - ✓ **American Translators Association (ATA)**
    http://bit.ly/T3-ATAAgree
  - ✓ **Association of Translators and Interpreters of Ontario (ATIO)**
    http://bit.ly/T3-ATIOAgree
  - ✓ **MegaDox**
    http://bit.ly/T3-MegaDox
  - ✓ **PEN America**
    http://bit.ly/T3-PenAgree

- ○ U.S. Government Paperwork
  - ✓ **1099**
    http://bit.ly/T3-1099
  - ✓ **W-9**
    http://bit.ly/T3-W9

- ○ Vocabulary Research
  - ✓ **Free Dictionary**
    http://bit.ly/T3-FreeDict
  - ✓ **Proz.com Kudoz**
    http://bit.ly/T3-ProzKudoz
  - ✓ **TermWiki**
    http://bit.ly/T3-TermWiki
  - ✓ **Translators Cafe Terms**
    http://bit.ly/T3-TCTerms
  - ✓ **Translators Cafe Glossaries**
    http://bit.ly/T3-TCGlossaries
  - ✓ **Urban Dictionary**
    http://bit.ly/T3-UrbanDict
  - ✓ **WikiWords**
    http://bit.ly/T3-Wikiwords

- ✓ **Word Reference**
  http://bit.ly/T3-WordReference
- ✓ **Your Dictionary**
  http://bit.ly/T3-YourDict

○ Volunteering as a Translator
- ✓ **Idealist**
  http://bit.ly/T3-Idealist
- ✓ **National Language Services Corp**
  http://bit.ly/T3-NatLangCorp
- ✓ **Rosetta Foundation**
  http://bit.ly/T3-RosettaFoundation
- ✓ **TED Talks Translators**
  http://bit.ly/T3-TEDTrans
- ✓ **Translations For Progress**
  http://bit.ly/T3-TransProg
- ✓ **Translators Without Borders**
  http://bit.ly/T3-TWB
- ✓ **UN Volunteers**
  http://bit.ly/T3-UNVolunteers
- ✓ **Volunteer Match**
  http://bit.ly/T3-VolMarch

○ Website and Blog Creation
- ✓ **Blogger**
  http://bit.ly/T3-Blogger
- ✓ **Fuel My Blog**
  http://bit.ly/T3-FuelBlog
- ✓ **GoDaddy**
  http://bit.ly/T3-GoDaddy
- ✓ **Google Sites**
  http://bit.ly/T3-GoogleSites
- ✓ **Homestead**
  http://bit.ly/T3-Homestead
- ✓ **HubPages**
  http://bit.ly/T3-HubPages

- ✓ iPages
  http://bit.ly/T3-iPages
- ✓ Joomla
  http://bit.ly/T3-Joomla
- ✓ LiveJournal
  http://bit.ly/T3-LiveJournal
- ✓ **Medium**
  http://bit.ly/T3-Medium
- ✓ **Network Solutions**
  http://bit.ly/T3-NetworkSolutions
- ✓ **SquareSpace**
  http://bit.ly/T3-SquareSpace
- ✓ **Tumblr**
  http://bit.ly/T3-Tumblr
- ✓ **Typepad**
  http://bit.ly/T3-TypePadCom
- ✓ **Web.com**
  http://bit.ly/T3-Web
- ✓ **Webs.com**
  http://bit.ly/T3-WebsCom
- ✓ **Weebly.com**
  http://bit.ly/T3-WeeblyCom
- ✓ **Wix.com**
  http://bit.ly/T3-WixCom
- ✓ **Wordpress.com**
  http://bit.ly/T3-WordpressCom
- ✓ **Wordpress.org**
  http://bit.ly/T3-WordpressOrg

- o **Wikipedia Pages for T&I Professionals**
  - ✓ **Comparative Literature**
    http://bit.ly/T3-WikiCompLit
  - ✓ **Computer-Assisted Translation Tools**
    http://bit.ly/T3-WikiCATs
  - ✓ **Copy Editing**
    http://bit.ly/T3-WikiCopyEd

- ✓ **Crowdfunding**
  http://bit.ly/T3-WikiCrowd
- ✓ **Digital Dictation**
  http://bit.ly/T3-WikiDictation
- ✓ **Interpreting**
  http://bit.ly/T3-Interpreting
- ✓ **Language**
  http://bit.ly/T3-WikiLang
- ✓ **Machine Translation**
  http://bit.ly/T3-WikiMT
- ✓ **Optical Character Recognition**
  http://bit.ly/T3-WikiOCR
- ✓ **Proofreading**
  http://bit.ly/T3-WikiProof
- ✓ **Social Networking**
  http://bit.ly/T3-WikiSocNet
- ✓ **Speech Recognition**
  http://bit.ly/T3-WikiSpeech
- ✓ **St. Jerome**
  http://bit.ly/T3-WikiJerome
- ✓ **Transcription Software**
  http://bit.ly/T3-WikiTransc
- ✓ **Translation**
  http://bit.ly/T3-WikiTrans
- ✓ **Translation Associations**
  http://bit.ly/T3-WikiTransAssoc
- ✓ **Translation Memory**
  http://bit.ly/T3-WikiTM
- ✓ **Translation Studies**
  http://bit.ly/T3-WikiTransStudies

EXTRAS

Image Credits

- Cover: "Click Click" by Tim Franklin Photography
  http://www.flickr.com/photos/58251661@N03/7254500880
- Cover and Back Cover: "Blue Tiles" by Patrick Hoesly
  http://www.flickr.com/photos/zooboing/8714972415
- Page 13: "USB Guys up to Mischief" by Andreas Brandmaier
  https://www.flickr.com/photos/brandmaier/4072900520
- Page 21: "Menace From The Land Before Color" by JD Hancock
  https://www.flickr.com/photos/jdhancock/4091338317
- Page 25: "Blanco" by Enrique Dans
  https://www.flickr.com/photos/edans/6673485073
- Page 41: "Calculating Taxes Up and Down" by Ken Teegardin
  https://www.flickr.com/photos/teegardin/5913069484
- Page 89: "Spinning Gears" by Brent 2.0
  https://www.flickr.com/photos/brentinoz/4221291984
- Page 139: "Research" by Nomadic Lass
  https://www.flickr.com/photos/nomadic_lass/6820209341
- Page 179: "The Best Days Are Not Planned" by Marcus Hansson
  http://www.flickr.com/photos/marcus_hansson/87885327
- Page 182: "Gina Bushnell" by UCSD Extension
  http://bit.ly/TI-UCSDExt
- Page 185: "Judy Jenner" by Sam Woodall
  http://fremonteaststudios.com
- Page 189: "Jennifer De La Cruz" by Danny Mariscal
  http://www.38photos.com
- Page 187: "iPhone Transparent Screen" by Enrique Dans
  https://www.flickr.com/photos/edans/1526393678
- Back Cover: "Author Image" by Rafa Lombardino
  http://ewordnews.com/profile

For more information and to see charts in full color
and a more legible version of the sample
resume and cover letter shown here, visit
http://www.RafaLombardino.com/tools

Made in the USA
San Bernardino, CA
13 April 2016